D1453975

Getting Ready for College Begins in Third Grade

Working Toward an Independent Future for Your Blind/Visually Impaired Child

Pre-K to Middle School

A volume in
Critical Concerns in Blindness

Series Editor
Edward C. Bell, *Louisiana Tech University*

Critical Concerns in Blindness

Edward C. Bell, Series Editor

Getting Ready for College Begins in Third Grade

Working Toward an Independent Future for Your Blind/Visually Impaired Child

Pre-K to Middle School

Carol Castellano

Information Age Publishing, Inc.
Charlotte, North Carolina • www.infoagepub.com

Library of Congress Cataloging-in-Publication Data

Castellano, Carol, 1951-
  Getting ready for college begins in third grade : working toward an
independent future for your blind/visually impaired child / by Carol Castellano.
    p. cm. — (Critical concerns in blindness)
  Includes bibliographical references.
    ISBN 978-1-61735-070-2 (papeback) — ISBN 978-1-61735-071-9 (hardcover) —
ISBN 978-1-61735-072-6 (e-book)
    1. Blind children—Education (Elementary)—United States. 2. Children with
visual disabilities—Education (Elementary)—United States. 3. Education—
Parent participation—United States. I. Title.
  HV1643.C37 2010
  649'.1511—dc22

                                                                    2010018431

Cover Design: Grace David
Cover Photo Editing: Jamie Iannuzzelli

Printed in the United States of America

To Doris Willoughby
and
Ruby Ryles

Your words of hope, inspiration, wisdom, and common sense
enabled me to see the possibilities for my daughter's life

CONTENTS

PREFACE

My daughter, totally blind and now a young adult, had the good fortune to be educated during a time of excellent teaching and full funding for special services in our state. Although we had our confrontations with the school system, especially at the beginning, by second grade her education was solidly on track. Now graduated from college, doing meaningful work, and applying to graduate school, I believe she and all parties involved would agree that her education was a success. So I started out with the belief that a blind/visually impaired child could receive a good education on a par with peers. I knew it could be done and I had some idea of how to do it.

Over the years, I became more and more active in the National Organization of Parents of Blind Children, advocating for families desperately seeking a decent education for their blind and visually impaired (VI) children. I began to notice that it was often in third or fourth grade when the education of a blind/VI student went off track. I also observed that, too many times, no one at the school was thinking in terms of getting it back on track. A blind/VI student's falling behind was just *accepted*! Students were moved along in the grades; students graduated. But they did not receive the same full education as their sighted classmates.

Was it blindness/visual impairment that was holding them back? I knew for sure it wasn't that. So I began to analyze what was going wrong in third and fourth grades and what could be done to remediate it or, better yet, prevent it. I also began to realize that what happened to the child in third grade—and before—could have a real impact on that child's future. Not only could it affect the quality of the rest of the child's education, but it could also determine whether or not the student would be on schedule to take courses like algebra and geometry, necessary to prepare for high-stakes tests such as the SAT and the ACT, which can play a major part in whether or not the student gets into a good college.

The first focus of the book is how to get the child's education on track and, if it has fallen off, how to create a workable plan to get it back on. The book also provides an overview of the factors that lead to a child's being ready to learn and the elements that are needed to make the education a success. (For step-by-step guides to education, please see *The Bridge to Braille: Reading and School Success for the Young Blind Child* and *Making It Work: Educating the Blind/Visually Impaired Student in the Regular School*. A step-by-step for parents on the blind/VI child's early development is in progress.) Thinking about how getting ready for college really did begin early in the child's education led me to contemplate the other areas in which a child would need competence in order to thrive in later life—independent living skills, independent movement and travel, social skills, and self-advocacy. And thus the book emerged.

I wanted to avoid education jargon and the trends, fashions, and buzz-words du jour, and focus instead on the larger perspective. The practices, policies, and laws may change, but the underlying challenges and obstacles facing blind/VI children in their education, such as low expectations and lack of opportunity to learn and master skills, remain the same. This book provides an *approach* to the development and education of blind/VI children, based on the idea of equal expectations and the right to equal opportunity. Through it, I hope to encourage parents to look toward the future without fear and to equip them with the information they need in order to raise their blind/VI child for an independent future. Good luck!

Carol Castellano
February 2010

ACKNOWLEDGMENTS

Where would we be without our dear colleagues, family, and friends who support and help us in our lives and work? I appreciate you all so much.

I am grateful to Eddie Bell, Barbara Cheadle, and Joe Ruffalo for their encouragement and unwavering support of this project and to all my Federation friends for always inspiring me.

My thanks go to Serena Cucco, Carol Forti, Stephanie Kieszak-Holloway, Denise Mackenstadt, Debbie Kent Stein, Patty Tumminello, and Laura Weber for their thoughtful comments on the chapters. Special thanks go to Barbara Shalit and Doris Willoughby for their careful reading of the manuscript and their invaluable ideas and suggestions. My deep appreciation goes to Joe Cutter, Sadako Vargas, and Doug Boone for their can-do attitude and creative ideas for independent movement and cane travel and for teaching me so much over the years.

To Laura, Stephanie, Richard Holloway, and Merry-Noel Chamberlain, I express my thanks for sharing their wonderful photos. I only wish we could have used them all! My gratitude goes also to Suzanne Shaffer for assistance with photos. I thank Adrienne, Anthony, Ashleah, Cody, Hailee, Helen, Jennifer, Joe, John, Kendra, Kyra, Lauren, Lindsay, Luke, Megan, Michael, RJ, Robbie, Serena, and Vivian for being their beautiful selves.

Thank you to Ellen and Mina for always being the best of friends. To Ed, Paul, Paulie, and especially Maria and Lynnie, I express amazement at their creativity and thanks for their hours of brainstorming. To them and all the fam—the Nunz, Barb and the Boys, Melanie, Johnny and Marisa,

Getting Ready for College Begins in Third Grade: Working Toward an Independent Future for Your Blind/Visually Impaired Child, pp. xi–xii

Donna and Richard, Dad, Annette and Cabell, Gina, all the kids—and especially my wonderful Billy, Serena, and John, I express my true love.

CHAPTER 1

HIGH EXPECTATIONS

We have so many hopes and dreams for our children. We want them to develop to their full potential. We want them to be able to do things for themselves and become contributing members of the household. We hope they will learn how to play and get along with others. We want them to learn well in school and eventually to do fulfilling work. We hope they will have a satisfying life, complete with family, friends, and fun.

Should these dreams be any different for our blind/visually impaired (VI) children? Must we lower our standards, our hopes, our expectations, our dreams? Absolutely not!

But how do we get there? How do we teach our blind/VI children? How can a blind/VI child develop and learn and grow? It's as easy as one, two, three:

1. Become aware of blind/VI people's achievements.
2. Raise your expectations.
3. Learn the techniques that blind/VI people use to accomplish tasks.

For example, have you read about the totally blind man who became a medical doctor in the early 1900s? One of the most respected physicians in the Chicago area, Dr. Jacob Bolotin, taught at the medical school, headed several hospital departments, and was a gifted diagnostician. Do you know that a blind man successfully climbed Mount Everest? In addition to reaching the summit of that great mountain in 2001, Erik Weihen-

Figure 1.1.   Our kids can make it to the top.

mayer is one of fewer than 100 mountaineers who have climbed the tallest peaks on every continent. Do you know that blind/VI people work in virtually every field, including education, engineering, biology, chemistry, physics, mechanics, government, legal services, social services, and even bee keeping?

Once we realize that blindness/visual impairment does not have to stop our children from achieving in school and career, and that blind/VI people go to college, get married, get jobs, raise families, volunteer in the community, and otherwise live completely normal lives, we also realize that we can and must raise our expectations for our blind/VI children.

Children will rise or fall to the bar we set. So why not set the bar high—as high as we would set it for any of our children? Expect that your child will learn the alphabet and how to count; expect your child to learn to share and take turns; expect your child to learn to behave. Expect your child to learn to read, do well in school, take part in gym class, join clubs, and play a musical instrument. Why not! And, if we expect these things of our children, our children will internalize the expectation and begin to expect things of themselves.

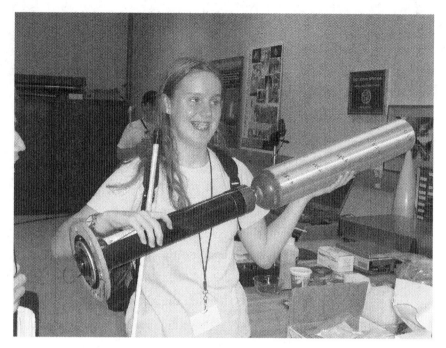

Figure 1.2.   The sky's the limit!

Once we know that all of the usual activities of life *can* be done, we just have to learn the tools and techniques that blind/VI people use to do them. We can join organizations and listservs and online groups to meet blind/VI people and learn from them. We can ask teachers and rehab professionals. We can read books and journals and articles to find out. It is up to us to set the stage for the child's success by learning the techniques and providing opportunities for our children to practice them. Enough practice will lead to competence and then mastery of the tasks. We can and should have expectations in every area: academics, social interaction, independence skills, self-care, independent movement, and travel.

What if your child is behind or delayed in some areas? Don't despair. Just make a plan: Choose a few goals; break each task down into steps; and take the time to practice, practice, practice. You will see results. All your hard work—and your child's—will be rewarded when you see your child filled with competence and confidence, and you will proudly watch as your son or daughter walks independently in line with the rest of the class in elementary school, plays along with everyone else in the band, moves confidently from classroom to classroom in a new school building, or walks across the stage to receive that eighth-grade diploma. You can feel proud of yourself, too, for successfully launching your child toward an independent future.

CHAPTER 2

ACADEMICS

INTRODUCTION

When things are going well, the blind/visually impaired child's education moves along full-speed-ahead, just as the education of the sighted child does. Teachers hold age-appropriate expectations for academics, behavior, and physical and social development, and provide timely intervention when an expectation is not met. Hopefully your child's education is following this path; if it is not, this chapter can help you figure out what's gone wrong, and how to get things back on track. If your child is just at the beginning of the education process, the chapter can help you get things going well right from the beginning and alert you to pitfalls to avoid.

GETTING ON TRACK FROM THE GET-GO

A detailed how-to on the early development of blind/VI children is the topic of another book, but here is an overview of what it takes to get the education of a blind/VI child on track right from the beginning and how any child—blind or sighted—gets to the point of being ready for school and formal learning.

Getting Ready for College Begins in Third Grade: Working Toward an Independent Future for Your Blind/Visually Impaired Child, pp. 5–24
Copyright © 2010 by Information Age Publishing
All rights of reproduction in any form reserved.

Developmental Experiences

In order to gain readiness for formal learning, children need *typical developmental experiences*. Through their experiences, children learn about themselves and the people, places, and things in the world around them. As these experiences accumulate, they form a knowledge base, which the child begins to understand, organize, and think about. This accumulation of information and understanding is the foundation on which formal learning is built. Many experiences go into gaining this readiness for learning, and these are, for the most part, the same for the blind/VI child as for the sighted child.

What does this look like in real life? It is the blind/VI infant experiencing the same kinds and amounts of movement and social interaction as the sighted infant; it is the blind/VI toddler moving about in the world, exploring, discovering, and finding out what things are out there and what can be done with them; it is the blind/VI preschooler getting plenty of physical activity, beginning to use language and get emotions under control, learning self-help skills, developing social relationships not only with adults, but also with other children, and learning concepts and the basics of academic work.

Take a look at the readiness expectations for a preschool or kindergarten in your community and you will see the kind of basic skills a child is expected to have upon entering school:

- The ability to interact with and learn from adults other than family members;
- The ability to interact with other children;
- The ability to share, take turns, and play cooperatively;
- The ability to sit still for a little while;
- The ability to pay attention for a little while;
- The ability to stay "on task" for a little while;
- The ability to follow simple directions;
- An understanding of the basic concepts that underlie formal learning; and
- Self-help skills such as eating a snack, using the bathroom, tying shoes, putting on a coat, and putting on a backpack.

The child who has been provided with typical developmental experiences will have age-appropriate understanding and skills and will come to school ready to learn. The child who is ready to learn will be able to be

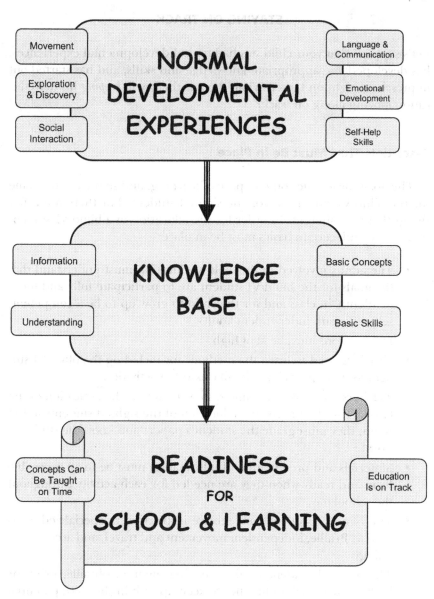

Figure 2.1.   Steps to an on-track education.

taught concepts at the same time as the other children in the class. The child who can be taught concepts at the same time as other children is a child whose education is on track.

STAYING ON TRACK

Let's suppose that your child has had typical developmental experiences, has developed age-appropriate knowledge and skills, and has started out in preschool right on target. What, then, is the key to *keeping* his/her education moving along on track?

Essentials That Must Be in Place

The goals, academic content, pace of learning, and so on, are the same for the blind/VI student as for the sighted student. But there are a few things that are different. In order for the education of a blind/VI student to be successful, certain basics must be in place:

- The adults involved in the child's education must understand that the goals for the blind/VI student are to participate fully and independently in class and for the child to grow up to be a competent, self-sufficient, independent adult.
- Expectations must be kept high.
- Teachers need to learn the methods for including the blind/VI student as a full participant in all classroom activities.
- Teachers must take the same responsibility for the education of the blind/VI student as for the education of the sighted students in the room; they must grade the student's papers and know the student's work.
- Materials and presentation of information must be in an accessible form and ready when they are needed for each activity throughout the school day.
- The blind/VI student must receive instruction in specialized areas such as Braille, independent movement and travel, and access technology.
- The blind/VI student needs a reading medium—braille, print, or both—which enables him/her to keep up with his/her own potential and with the class.
- Classroom teachers need (a) to be familiar with the materials, tools, and techniques the blind/VI child will use and (b) to understand that they are the equivalents to skills and tools sighted people use.
- School personnel must respect the cane and encourage the student's independent mobility.

Figure 2.2.   Working with math manipulatives.

- There must be good communication and flexibility among all parties involved—teachers, student, parents, teacher of the blind/VI, Individualized Education Plan (IEP) team, administrators.
- Each IEP goal should have an instructional guide listing the special tools and techniques needed to reach the goal.
- The IEP should have an explicit goal of independence so that the student can become independent in the classroom and in all areas.
- The team must build in a timeline for independence; over time, the student must become more independent and need less assistance; the adults must make this come to pass.

(For a full discussion of setting up the education of the blind/VI child, please see the book *Making It Work: Educating the Blind/Visually Impaired Student in the Regular School*.)

Danger Areas

The blind/VI child is vulnerable to many well-meaning but mistaken beliefs and actions on the part of the many sighted adults in his/her life.

Figure 2.3.   A student reads to her classmates.

One of the most typical—and most dangerous—is overprotection. The typical sighted person is unaware that blind/VI people have tools and techniques that enable them to accomplish tasks safely and efficiently. Well-meaning adults often keep a child from doing a task, thinking that they are providing necessary protection. For example, they might keep a child from approaching a stairway or not permit him/her to travel down the hallway alone. As the parent, you will probably learn the techniques of blindness/visual impairment along with your child. Make sure your child gets plenty of time to practice these skills, and then teach others around you about them so that the adults in your child's life will not inadvertently be overprotective.

A related danger area involves the consequences of low expectations. Chances are, your child's teachers will not know initially that your child can be expected to achieve academically at the same level as sighted peers of similar cognitive ability. You will probably need to take the lead in acquainting teachers with the accomplishments of high-achieving blind persons so that they will be able to develop appropriately high expectations for your child.

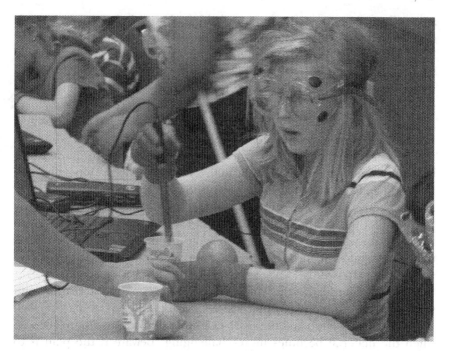

Figure 2.4.   Performing a science experiment.

Another typical area of vulnerability for the blind/VI child is that people will be all too willing to do things for the child, long after he/she should be doing them independently. Because of low expectations and lack of knowledge about techniques, it may never even occur to school staff that the child could learn to do the various tasks. *Learned dependence* will be the result. You will have to keep an eye on things to make sure that teachers, aides, and other staff allow your child age-appropriate autonomy and growth and that your child does not come to expect that others will always be doing tasks for him/her.

Reading and Writing Medium

Another extremely important area to pay attention to is making sure that the child has a reading and writing medium that will not only serve him/her now—in preschool, kindergarten, and the primary grades—but will take him/her into the future—through middle school, high school, and college. It may seem strange to think about getting ready for college when your child is so young, but the fact is that the child who has learned practical and efficient methods for reading and writing from the beginning won't ever have to take precious time out in the future to remediate and will be able to keep up with the class throughout the school years.

Look into the near future; think about third grade, when the print gets smaller and the paragraphs longer. How about fourth grade, when the number of letters and syllables per word increase and the paragraphs become longer and more complicated? Now think about long division, fractions, and decimals. Move on in your thoughts to high-school algebra and geometry. Your child needs a medium that will allow him/her to easily handle all of this math. Next, think about that darkened lecture hall with the professor who will hold students responsible for the content of the lecture. Your child will need an effective, efficient way to take notes and review them afterwards.

Make absolutely sure your child receives instruction in the reading and writing medium (or media) that will enable him/her not only to do well when the print is large and the math examples simple, but also to keep up when the material becomes more challenging. Beware if the plan is to switch to recorded books—these DO NOT develop literacy skills. Don't let anyone convince you that "children with visual impairments read at a slower rate," or "it's typical for blind/VI kids to be behind," or "your daughter can go into the resource room where the pace is slower and she can get more personal attention," or "we can make accommodations for your son's eyesight—he will only have to do enough math problems to demonstrate proficiency." *Not one of these so-called accommodations will teach your child how to keep up in an age-appropriate environment. Your child deserves better, so don't get caught in the trap!*

Partially sighted children can use so much energy just trying to see that they don't have full mental energy to apply to the academic task in front of them. For a variety of reasons, teachers of the blind/VI often do not suggest nonvisual alternatives, such as Braille, for these children. But don't be afraid of nonvisual skills. When added to your child's usable vision, they can make a real difference in the child's independence, academics, and even social life. Asking our legally blind children to do 100% of life's tasks visually when they only have 10% or less of normal vision is just plain crazy! Instead of sentencing them to fatigue, poor self-image, and school failure, offer them the chance for competence, confidence, and success by adding nonvisual tools and skills to their repertoire.

Aiming for Success

If your child is receiving instruction in the special skills of blindness/ visual impairment; if classroom teachers and other school staff learn enough about those skills to respect them, encourage their use, and help the student progress in them; if materials are accessible and ready when needed; if an independence plan is in place; and if the child is encouraged and expected to make age-appropriate progress in all areas, *then the education of that child should be a success*!

WHY DOES THE EDUCATION OF THE BLIND/VI STUDENT GO OFF TRACK?

In my experience, the typical time for the education of the blind/VI student to fall off track is third grade for the Braille user and fourth grade for the large-print user.

For the Braille User

For the Braille user, the difficulty usually surfaces in the area of math. Now, I want to be clear: *Math need be no more a problem for a blind/VI student than for a sighted student*. So why is it typical for math to be a problem area for the blind/VI student? I believe it is due to a combination of factors. First, there is a common misconception (often heard even among Braille teachers) that Nemeth Code, the system for writing math in Braille, is difficult. Because of this belief (and perhaps because the teacher him/herself never mastered the code), the teaching of Nemeth Code and the teaching of math might be delayed. The student may be able to follow along in first and second grades, when the math is very basic, and for a while may be able to do all the computation in his/her head, perhaps with a teacher or aide "helpfully" writing down the answers the student calculates. But eventually, the student starts falling behind in learning math concepts.

Here is another typical scenario: Due to low expectations, the student is never held to normal classroom standards and is not really expected to learn the material. In either case, by third grade, when both the concepts and the computations have become more complicated, the student is lost. A typical downward spiral ensues: Instead of realizing that the child has never been taught an efficient method to do math on paper or perhaps has never even seen math on paper, the team begins to suspect a learning disability. Finding a competent person to do the testing takes months.

Before you know it, the student has lost another year in school and the hole he/she must dig out of is that much deeper.

Reading can also become a problem area for the Braille user, again, not because reading in Braille is difficult, but because of other circumstances. For example, if the student is not receiving enough instruction time in Braille, he/she will not be able to keep up with the class's progress. If materials are not ready in accessible form for the whole school day, the student misses out on the many literacy opportunities the sighted children are receiving. In addition, a good deal of coordination is required in the early grades so that the child learns the code, the classroom teacher understands how to include the child in reading instruction, and the child's materials are ready when needed in accessible form. If too many glitches occur in any of these areas, the child will pay the price.

For the Print User

For the print user, the problem usually surfaces in fourth grade, when the print in the textbooks gets smaller, the words longer, and the paragraphs more dense. The student begins to have trouble reading passages in language arts, science, and social studies, and has difficulty deciphering math signs and symbols. His/her handwriting is painstaking and slow and he/she has difficulty trying to read it back. The student begins to take longer and longer to get assignments done and starts having trouble keeping up with the class. After reading, the child's eyes are red and teary; neck strain, headaches, and eye fatigue appear. The downward spiral begins. Teachers cut down assignments; expectations fall. The child begins to avoid reading tasks and maybe even loses interest in school. Teachers suspect laziness, or perhaps a learning disability. The student might be placed in a resource room where there are fewer students and the pace is slower. Now, mind you, none of this is because the child cannot understand the material presented; it is solely because he/she cannot read fast, easily, and comfortably enough to keep up with the classroom pace.

WHAT TO DO IF THINGS HAVE GONE OFF TRACK

If your child's education has gone off track, there are logical steps that you and the rest of the education team can take to put things right again. Through a methodical assessment of the various elements of the child's program, the team can pinpoint the area or areas that need to be rectified.

Is This a Learning Disability?

If a blind/VI student is having difficulties in school subjects, often the teacher or someone on the IEP team begins to suspect a learning disability. Several factors make it tricky to determine if a blind/VI student really has a learning disability:

- First, very few educators have experience in testing blind/VI students for learning disabilities.
- Second, what appears to be a learning difficulty can be the result of several other possibilities having nothing to do with an actual learning disability:

    o The student has not received adequate instruction in the subject;
    o The student has not received adequate instruction in the Braille code;
    o Instructional materials or the presentation of information are not accessible;
    o The child does not have a reading medium that allows him/her to keep up with classroom instruction; and
    o Any combination of the above.

The conclusion that the blind/VI child must have a learning disability is often reached too fast—before assessing and correcting other issues—and often without real evidence. Make sure the team is aware of the other factors that must also be assessed before the determination of a learning disability can be reliably made.

If evaluation results indicate the presence of a verifiable, actual learning disability, then the next step is to modify the education plan by adding appropriate techniques and accommodations for that learning disability. A useful way to determine what those techniques and accommodations should be is for the team to think about *what they would recommend for a sighted student* who presented with the same issues. Then, with the assistance of the teacher of the blind/VI, adapt these accommodations wherever needed for blindness/visual impairment, with Braille, large print, tactile or bold print materials, hands-on or close-up presentation, verbal description, et cetera.

Math Remediation Plan

To create a math remediation plan, baseline data must be collected in all the areas that might be affecting the child's math performance. The first step is to get a good sense of the child's present math skills. The school will have math assessment tools available for this purpose. Your child's teacher of the blind/VI could assist with the testing if needed. If the school's math program includes monthly or chapter assessments, looking at those results can reveal problem areas.

Assess Math Skills

The team would need to get baseline information in the following areas:

- The child's understanding of math concepts, from the basics on up to grade-level concepts;
- The child's ability to do math computation in his/her head;
- The child's ability to perform math calculations that are read to him/her;
- The child's ability to read and write math on paper, from the basics on up to grade-level math;
- The child's math problem-solving skills; and
- If applicable, the child's ability to use math manipulatives and tools (see the section, "Determine Accessibility of Materials and Presentation," below).

Assess Braille Skills

For many Braille users, what looks like a math difficulty is really the result of inadequately developed Braille skills. The child may be able to do math "in his/her head," but may not have been taught how to read or set up examples on paper. Therefore, the child's level of skill in reading and writing math in Braille must be evaluated. The child's ability to read and write literary Braille (the Braille used for reading and writing other than math) might need to be checked as well.

The team would need to collect information about the following:

- Has the child been taught to recognize the various math signs in Braille?
- Has the child been taught to write the math signs (including proper spacing) in Braille?
- Has the child been taught efficient methods to set up math examples on paper?
- Evaluate the child's ability to *read* math in Braille, from the basics on up to grade-level math.
- Evaluate the child's ability to *write* math in Braille, from the basics on up to grade-level math.

Determine Accessibility of Materials and Presentation

The final area in which information must be collected is the accessibility of both materials and the presentation of information. Again, what might look like a problem with math ability may really be a problem with the tools the child is being asked to work with.

Regarding materials and the presentation of information, the team should ask questions like these:

- Does the child need math manipulatives (small objects used for instruction and homework in math)?
- Are the manipulatives the child is working with tactilely coded? Are they being presented in a tray or box so that the child is able to keep track of them? Do they stay together for counting or comparison purposes?
- Are they representative of the concept being taught? Do they work?
- Are appropriate manipulatives ready when the lesson is being taught?
- Is the child getting adequate time to work with the materials in order to learn and practice the concept?
- Is the classroom teacher using accessible language? (For example, instead of saying, "Fold the paper this way," is he or she saying, "Fold the paper lengthwise"?)
- Is there adequate coordination between the classroom teacher and the teacher of the blind/VI?
- Is there opportunity for the teacher of the blind/VI to teach new Nemeth Code signs and symbols in advance of their appearance in the math book?

- Is there opportunity for the teacher of the blind/VI to show the child how to use new tools and equipment (for example, a tactile ruler or meter stick)?
- Is the child getting time to practice with the new items?

Creating the Math Remediation Plan

There are three main sections of a math remediation plan—content, planning who will teach the content, and creating a timeline for the plan.

Content

First, teachers need to decide on content. Remediation content will probably be a combination of the three areas of assessment discussed above: math skills, Braille skills, and improving materials and presentation. A specific, sequential plan will give the student the best chance of catching up.

Who Will Teach?

Next, decide who will teach the content. For example, the school may have a basic skills teacher who could work on the math; the teacher of the blind/VI could work on the Braille skills and materials (in coordination with the classroom teacher); the teacher of the blind/VI could work with the classroom teacher on making the presentation accessible; and the parents could give the child practice using tools and materials at home.

The Timeline

Finally, create a timeline for the catch-up period. The timeline will have two parts: The first part is a schedule listing when the student will receive the instruction in math and in Braille each day and each week. The second part uses the "work backwards" approach: Look ahead to the goal, figure out how much time there is between then and now, and then plan what would have to be taught when, in order to cover all the material by the goal date.

Here is an example. The child is in third grade; it is the month of January; the child's math skills are at the mid-first-grade level; and the goal is for the student to be caught up by fourth grade. You would look ahead to fourth grade and figure out how many months were left until then. For this child, there would be eight months, if the child would be able to continue catching up over the summer. This means about sixteen months' worth of work would have to be made up in about eight months' time. The team would then have to determine what content would have to be covered each week and each month in order to make the plan work.

How fast the remediation can proceed will depend on many factors, including the child's learning ability and style, the amount and complexity of the material to be studied, scheduling possibilities, et cetera. Aim

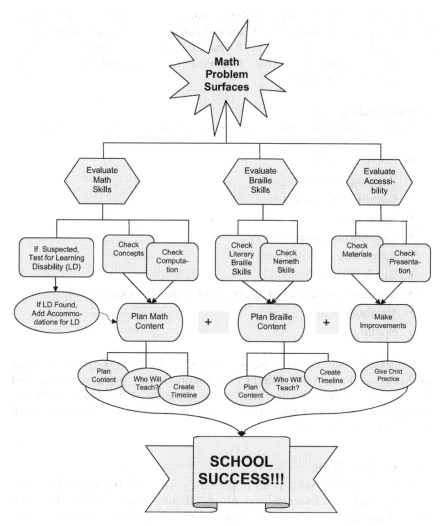

Figure 2.5.   Math remediation plan.

for a timetable that is optimistic enough to push the child along, yet takes into account a realistic learning pace. In this way, both teachers and child will encounter success.

Remember, the ultimate timeline is for the child to be ready to take algebra and geometry in the appropriate grade so that he/she will be on track for college entrance exams and college.

Reading Remediation Plan

Creating a remediation plan for reading follows the same pattern as creating a plan for math. The team will collect baseline data in the areas affecting the child's reading performance. The school will have assessment tools available to do this. The teacher of the blind/VI could assist with the testing if needed.

Assess Reading Skills

The team would need to get information in areas such as the following:

- Decoding skills;
- Reading strategies;
- Comprehension skills;
- Inference;
- Determining importance;
- Extracting information;
- Reading speed;
- Fluency (reading quickly, accurately, and with expression);
- Vocabulary; and
- Spelling.

Remember that the team must assess what the child is able to read on his/her own. Do not be satisfied with someone telling you that he/she does very well when read to or when using listening skills. These skills are indeed very important for the blind/VI child to develop, but he/she still needs to be able to read.

Assess Braille Skills

Assessing Braille skills is an important part of solving a problem with reading, since what looks like a reading difficulty can actually be the product of inadequately developed Braille skills. The team should ask questions like the following:

- Is the child getting enough Braille instruction to fully learn the code and keep up with the class?
- Has the child learned to read all the contractions and punctuation marks?
- Has the child learned to write all the contractions and punctuation marks?
- Has the child been taught efficient reading techniques?
- Has the child been taught efficient writing techniques?
- Has the child been taught efficient ways to handle worksheets and books?

Assess the Reading Medium

Are the child's difficulties due to the reading medium in which he/she is being instructed? Ask questions like these:

- Is the child able to read grade-level passages in a timely fashion?
- Is the child's reading speed and fluency on a par with his/her own potential? With that of peers?
- Is the child able to read grade-level passages without fatigue, eye strain, headaches, neck strain, et cetera?
- Is the child able to take and read back his/her own notes?
- Is the child making grade-level progress in literacy skills?

Check Materials and Classroom Issues

Another area in which to collect information pertains to materials and any classroom issues that might be affecting the child's reading.

- Is the child receiving good quality Braille? (This is particularly important for the youngest children.)
- Is there good coordination between the classroom teacher and the teacher of the blind/VI, so that new Braille signs and contractions can be taught in advance of classroom reading instruction?
- Has the classroom teacher received training on how to include blind/VI student in class reading and writing instruction?
- Is the student getting the same opportunities to write as classmates?
- Is the classroom teacher aware of the materials and tools that are available?

Creating the Reading Remediation Plan

If the data that are collected point to the need to change the reading medium from print to Braille, or to use a combination of print and Braille, a schedule will need to be created for beginning instruction in Braille. The teacher of the blind/VI will suggest a plan for incorporating the new medium into the child's classroom work and homework.

Next, address any classroom issues identified in the assessment process above.

Then plan the three sections of the reading remediation plan: planning content, determining who will teach the content, and creating a timeline for the plan.

Content

First, decide on what material needs to be taught. This is usually a combination of Braille and reading skills. As with a plan for math remediation, a specific, sequential plan will provide the best chance for the student to catch up.

Who Will Teach?

The person who works on reading with the child will probably need to work closely with the teacher of the blind/VI so that the student can make the most progress.

The Timeline

As with the math plan, the timeline for a reading remediation plan will have two parts. The first part will define when the student will receive the instruction in reading and in Braille each day and each week. The second part will use the "work backwards" approach: Look ahead to the goal, figure out how much time there is between then and now, and then plan what has to be taught when, in order to cover all the material by the goal date.

Here is an example for reading. The child is in fourth grade; it is the month of March; the child is reading at the beginning second-grade level; and the goal is for the child to be caught up by the end of fifth grade. Look ahead to the end of fifth grade and figure out how many months are left until then. For this child, there would be fifteen months, if the child would be able to continue catching up over the summer. This means about twenty-four months' worth of work would have to be made up in about fifteen months' time. The team would then have to determine what content would have to be covered each week and each month in order to make the plan work.

Again, as with math, how fast the remediation can proceed will depend on factors such as the child's learning ability and style, the amount of material to be studied, and scheduling possibilities. A timetable that pushes the child along, yet takes into account a realistic learning pace, will generate success for both teachers and child.

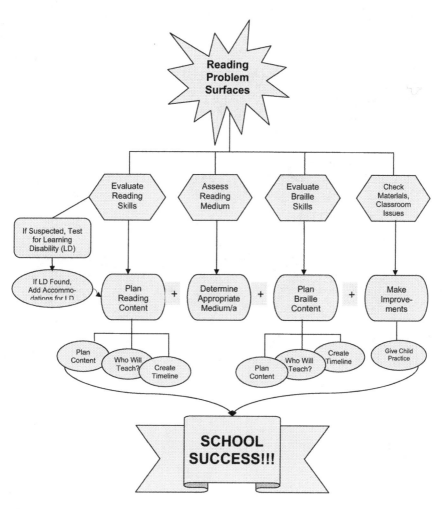

Figure 2.6.   Reading remediation plan.

ON TRACK FOR THE FUTURE

Once on grade level—or above!—in reading and math, your child will be ready for advanced work and will be on track for taking college preparatory courses in eighth grade and high school. Equipped with a solid foundation, he or she will be able to look forward to the excitement and academic challenges of the upper grades with competence and confidence.

CHAPTER 3

INDEPENDENT LIVING SKILLS

INTRODUCTION

One of the most important responsibilities we have as parents is to teach our children the skills they will need in order to take care of themselves when they grow up. This is as true for our blind/VI children as it is for our sighted children. If we don't fulfill this responsibility, we deny our children the chance to live fully independently. If we do our job, then we start our blind/VI children out with a firm foundation and an ability to handle the activities of their own lives equal to that of their sighted peers.

THE TRICKS

There are a few tricks to it. First of all, if you are a sighted parent, you probably do not know the techniques that blind/VI people use to accomplish the various tasks of everyday life. Secondly, it is very easy to continue to do jobs *for* our blind/VI children long after the age at which they should be doing them for themselves. Why do we do this? There are many possible reasons—there might be a tendency to baby the child; perhaps it is misplaced compassion, feeling sorry for the child and not wanting to add to the child's "burden"; maybe the child has delays in development and you just haven't gotten there yet; maybe you don't know how a blind/VI

Getting Ready for College Begins in Third Grade: Working Toward an Independent Future for Your Blind/Visually Impaired Child, pp. 25–38

person would do the task; or the classic reason—it's faster and easier just to do the job yourself.

Whatever the reason, we owe it to our blind/VI children—as we do to all of our children—to teach them to take care of themselves. Here are the keys:

- Assume that the job can be done.
- Find out how blind/VI people do the task (by the way, there is usually more than one way). Ask a teacher of the blind/VI, or better yet, ask a blind/VI person!
- Stay on an age-appropriate path (or a stage-appropriate path, if the child has delays).

One way to think about it is to ask yourself what you would have your child doing at that stage if he or she were sighted. Think back to your own childhood—what did your parents expect of you at various ages? What tasks were you responsible for? Aim for at least that level of knowledge and competence.

TIME AWARENESS AND TIME MANAGEMENT

In order to be independent in the future, children must learn to accomplish tasks within the usual amount of time allotted. Some children seem to be born with a day planner in their head, knowing exactly what they will do that day and how much time each task is likely to take. If your blind/VI child is not blessed with an innate sense of time management, you can help him/her develop it. There are two parts to the development of this skill: (1) time awareness—knowing what time it is and being aware of the feeling of time passing, and (2) moving in a fast enough manner to get the task done in the time allotted.

Developing Time Awareness

Some children are operating on common time—they have a sense of time passing; they are aware of how fast others accomplish various tasks; they move fast enough to get the job done in the usual amount of time. Other children seem to be operating on personal time—they seem oblivious to the passage of time; they don't pay attention to how fast they or others are moving; they move at their own—snail-like—pace. If you've got one of these little pokey ones, here are some ideas for developing time awareness:

- Talk with your child about time and the passage of time.
- Teach your child how to tell time; Braille practice clocks are available from the American Printing House for the Blind (APH).
- Have your child wear a watch and periodically ask him/her what time it is. Get a Braille watch, if possible—since a talking watch makes noise, it will be less useful in the classroom, another place where the pokey ones need to stay aware of time.
- Put talking clocks in various rooms of the house.
- Play games that will help your child learn what various durations of time feel like. For example, ask your child how long he/she thinks it will take to go up the stairs and back down again or to eat breakfast or to put on shoes and socks. Then check the time, have your child do the task, and check the time again.

Getting Faster

You'll need to be pretty involved for a while as you work on training your child to move faster. Here are a few ideas:

- Figure out which tasks are taking too long, and put a clock in rooms where those activities take place. Have your child check the time before and after tasks.
- Ask your child, "How much time do you think has gone by? Let's check." Or ask, "How much time do you think that's going to take? Let's time it."
- Use a timer. Play "Beat the Clock."
- Do the task at the same time as your child is doing it and talk about your progress. For example, brush your teeth while your child brushes his/hers. "Okay, I've got the toothpaste on my brush. How're you doing?" "I just finished brushing front and sides and back. How are you doing?"
- Have a race.

Racing Through

If you have a child who speeds through every task and is not thorough enough, that's a different issue! Following are some ideas from teacher of the blind/VI Doris Willoughby for the child who needs to develop patience and attention to detail (personal communication, January 10, 2010).

- Time awareness is important to the child who "finishes" too fast, too. The child needs to become aware of the pace at which others are moving.

- Analyze how long it would take to do the job thoroughly or well, or time yourself or someone else doing the task in the usual amount of time.

- Talk with your child about the amount of time the task takes the average person. Time your child doing the task. Discuss the comparison with your child.

- Have your child rate how well the task was done. Was it satisfactory on the first try? Discuss with your child that the task cannot be considered complete until it is actually finished fully and appropriately.

- With input from your child, chart how long the task took and how well it was done on the first try.

- Analyze the steps involved with completing the task. Make sure your child really understands what is involved and expected.

- Braille out a list of the steps for your child to follow. He/she can make sure each step is done and done well enough before moving on to the next one.

- Is your child enjoying the attention he/she gets by doing a job too fast or poorly? If so, minimize the attention he/she receives while doing the task and maximize it when the task is done appropriately.

- Is there something about the job that the child really hates that makes him/her want to get through the task as quickly as possible? If so, can this aspect be modified in some way to make the task less unpleasant?

- Does the child perceive a "reward" when he/she gets done fast? Can you manipulate the situation so that the reward does not apply? For example, don't have the child do the chore right before his/her favorite TV program.

- Set a reasonable minimum time that must be devoted to the task. If the child "finishes" early, he/she may not leave or play. The child must stay and "keep thinking about whether a part or parts of the task could be done better." When the time is up (not before), check the child's work. If the task has not been completed correctly, set another minimum time he/she must spend before you will check the work.

- If your child is using partial sight for a task such as homework, could he/she be rushing through because he/she knows a headache will be coming after a certain amount of time? If this is the case, the remedy is to learn Braille!

SELF-CARE

Blind children can learn self-care skills in the same sequence as sighted children, and you can use any parenting book as a guide. Cover all the usual areas:

- Make sure your little one can wash hands and face and brush teeth.
- Make sure your older child learns how to wash his/her hair and bathe or shower independently.
- Teach your child to dress and undress independently.

Table Manners and Eating Skills

Your young blind/VI child needs to learn all the usual table manners that you would teach any of your children (more on this in Chapter 5: Social Awareness and Social Skills). In addition to manners, you may need to devote some extra attention to eating skills.

Expect your child to learn to eat neatly and to use utensils—including a knife—in the usual fashion. Avoid letting your child eat with his/her hands any longer than is age-appropriate. Don't let your child put his/her face into the bowl in order to see the food. Instead, teach alternative methods of discerning what is on the plate that enable him or her to keep his/her head up, such as surveying the plate with the fork. The child can also ask what is on the plate and where it is located (not usually necessary at home, where it is likely the child knows what's for dinner, but a useful method when eating at a restaurant or at someone else's house).

Food Overboard!

Expect some food spilling over the edge of the plate when your child is first learning to eat with utensils, but don't let this go on for too long (again, aim for the same point at which most children master keeping the food on their plate). Show your child how to scoop and pierce in different areas and how to keep from inadvertently pushing the food off the edge of the plate. Have your older child check the table around the plate to monitor his/her own neatness level. If your child is a messy one, perhaps you could offer incentives for meals eaten without leaving spillage or debris around the dish.

Knives and Cutting

If your child is having trouble using a knife, here are a few suggestions:

- Go back to basics—roll out some clay or play-dough "snakes" for the child to practice with. Using regular metal utensils, your child can practice piercing and holding the play food with a fork and cutting with a knife.
- Make sure your child is holding his/her elbows up while attempting to cut.
- Observe blind/VI adults to see the methods they use to cut food.

You can also shape clay into a pie wedge and have your child practice the technique of holding a fork horizontally to cut off a piece of food.

The Rest of the Story
Be sure your child learns other table techniques, such as using a napkin, sprinkling salt and pepper, spreading butter, and passing dishes to others. Teach your child to pour a drink and to get a drink of water from the faucet.

Last, but not least, eating is a social activity. Learning to take part in dinner conversation is another of those skills that has implications for the future, when your child will be eating in the school cafeteria and the college dining hall, and maybe someday having lunch with the boss. Your blind/VI child should be a regular part of dinner conversation—not dominating, but not invisible either—and needs to learn the usual basics: Face the person who is speaking or to whom you are speaking; speak between bites; don't speak with your mouth full. Just think back to what your parents taught you and pass it on. (For more on conversation skills, see Chapter 5: Social Awareness and Social Skills).

Cooking Without Looking ... Well, not Exactly Cooking ...

Observe what sighted children your child's age are able to do in the kitchen and teach your child at least the basic skills:

- Preparing a bowl of cereal (pouring the cereal; pouring the milk);
- Making toast;
- Spreading butter and spreads;
- Making a sandwich;
- Using the microwave (adapt with Braille on clear tape);
- Getting a drink from the faucet;
- Pouring a drink;
- Opening a juice box or can;

- Making an instant drink;
- Cutting up fruit; and
- Opening snack boxes and bags.

Figure 3.1. Cooking skills are important for an independent future.

If your child expresses a real interest in cooking and baking, be sure to get in touch with a blind/VI adult and look online to discover the many simple methods that blind/VI chefs use to successfully prepare meals and desserts.

Clothing and Dressing

Your little one will learn to dress and undress in the usual sequence—undressing (easier) before dressing (harder), easy clothing before more difficult clothing. But do expect him or her to learn it all, including buttons, snaps, zippers, Velcro, buckles, et cetera. Expect your preschooler to learn how to put on a jacket and zip it up and to hang it on a hook or hanger after taking it off. Expect your child to learn how to tie shoes. If your child is having difficulty with any of the basic tasks, try breaking them down into very small steps and teaching each step one at a time in sequence.

Danger Area

Blind children are very vulnerable to adults continuing to do tasks such as zipping up a jacket or tying shoes *long after* the usual age for such assistance instead of teaching the child how to do it. It is critically important for parents to (1) keep this in mind in order not to fall into the trap themselves, and (2) insist that other adults in the child's life—loving, well-meaning relatives, teachers, aides, et cetera—not do it either.

Choosing Clothing

Though your child may not visually see the clothing he or she is wearing, it is still important for him/her to learn about clothing colors, patterns, and styles, so that he/she will have a store of information similar to sighted friends. Here are some of the things to teach your child:

- The idea of light and dark shades of a color (and which laundry hamper they should go in);
- The idea of patterns and solids and what various patterns look like;
- What colors are considered to go with other colors;
- What words or pictures might be on clothing;
- What clothing is appropriate for the weather; and
- What clothing is appropriate for the activity.

When your child is young, you will likely be the one picking out the styles and colors and purchasing the outfits. As your child grows older, be aware of current clothing styles so that your child can wear clothing simi-lar to peers. Many children develop an interest in clothing and some come to have a style of their own. If your child is one of those *not* very interested in style or fashion, then work toward developing at least recog-nition of the fact that in our society, our level of cleanliness and grooming are important and have an effect on those around us.

Labeling Clothing

Your child needs a way to label clothing so that he/she can put together matching outfits and eventually get the worn clothing into the correct laundry basket. Blind/VI adults use many different methods to label and keep track of their clothing; here are a few ideas:

- For labeling
  - Use Braille/large print color tags that can be sewn or pinned into clothing.
  - Use one of the tactile symbol systems available for purchase.
  - Make your own Braille labels using a Braille label maker and Teflon tape.
  - Use one of the systems above along with a paper list of possible outfit combinations.
- For keeping track of clothing and outfits
  - Hang outfits together on the same hanger.
  - Place items of the same color together in the closet or in draw-ers.
  - Put school outfits in one drawer and play outfits in another.
- Put laundry bags or containers in your child's room; label one "lights" and one "darks."

ORGANIZATION SKILLS

Your child's ability to keep organized in general is a skill that will be important at every stage of his/her education, from preschool through college. Start your child out right by getting his/her toy and play area organized. Label shelves and drawers and teach your child to put things back where they belong. As your child gets older, involve him or her in the planning of what will go where. This will enable your child to organize clothing, books, papers, recreational items, et cetera at home, at camp, and eventually in a college dorm.

Figure 3.2.   Include your blind/VI child in household tasks and chores.

Figure 3.3.   A child orders for herself at a restaurant.

CHORES

Your blind/VI child should take part in household chores, just like any of your other children. Again, there are a few tricks to it:

- Aim for following an age-appropriate path.
- Learn the techniques that blind/VI people use to accomplish the tasks.
- Teach the tasks in a step-by-step manner.

Most children start with basic jobs such as setting and clearing the table, loading and unloading the dishwasher, helping put groceries away, putting clean clothes back into drawers, and taking out the recycling and garbage. Below is a method for parents to ensure that the child learns to do the common household tasks that lead to an independent future. Remember to find out how a blind/VI person accomplishes the tasks when you get to those chores that are less obvious for a sighted parent to figure out.

Getting an Overview

A simple way to get an overview of the tasks that your child needs to learn is to get a pad of paper and go from room to room in your house. In each room, look around and list the jobs that would need to be done in order to maintain the room. A child, of course, will not be doing all of these tasks at a young age, but thinking ahead to the various skills your child will need in the future will help you stay on track with teaching your child the skills. Table 3.1 provides an example of how such a list might look.

GOING TO THE STORE

One more important area in which to give your child practice for a future of independence takes place outside the home—going to the store. This wonderful activity involves many skills: independent mobility, social interaction, making choices, and handling money. Practice together before your child goes solo, guiding your child toward noticing the sounds, landmarks, and other clues he/she can use to accomplish the task independently. Before the excursion, give your child practice in asking how much an item costs, determining whether or not he/she has enough money to buy it, and figuring out what change he/she should receive. Get your child a wallet and have him/her practice putting money in and taking it out.

Table 3.1.   Chore Chart

Kitchen

__ Wipe crumbs off table	__ Wash counter
__ Wash table	__ Put out fresh dish cloth
__ Check chair for crumbs	__ Clean sink
__ Clean up a spill	__ Clean stove
__ Sweep floor	__ Clean oven
__ Use dust pan & brush	__ Load & unload dishwasher
__ Wash floor	__ Put soap in dishwasher
__ Wipe crumbs off counter	__ Wash dishes & pots

Bedroom

__ Make bed	__ Put sheets on bed
__ Take sheets off bed	__ Keep clothing organized
__ Wash, dry, fold sheets	__ Keep shoes organized

Bathroom

__ Clean sink and mirror	__ Shake out rugs
__ Wash toilet	__ Dust windowsill & shelves
__ Clean tub and shower	__ Wash & dry towels & rugs
__ Change towels	__ Wash floor

General

__ Sweep	__ Dust
__ Use dust pan & brush	__ Turn lights on & off
__ Vacuum	

Pet Care

__ Feed pet	__ Add fresh litter
__ Put out fresh water	__ Walk dog
__ Clean out litter box	__ Pick up after dog

Miscellaneous

__ Answer phone	__ Make change
__ Take message	__ Sew a button
__ Lock & unlock door	__ Iron on a patch

Outdoors

__ Bring in mail	__ Pull trash cans to and from curb
__ Bring in newspaper	__ Wash car
__ Do yard work	__ Shovel snow

PLUGGING IN

Make sure your child knows a safe method for plugging in electric cords. Show him/her the difference between two-pronged and three-pronged plugs and how to place them safely into outlets. If you are using a power strip, let your child examine it and learn how to use it. At the age-appropriate time, give your child the responsibility for remembering to charge his/her cell phone, notetaker, and other devices. Make sure he/she is learning how to insert the various cords and storage devices into computers, notetakers, et cetera.

ON THE ROAD TO INDEPENDENCE

Now go ahead and pat yourself on the back. Enjoy the feeling of pride as you watch your child gain skill, learn and master tasks, and begin to take age-appropriate responsibility for him or herself. You've started your child on the road to an independent life.

CHAPTER 4

INDEPENDENT MOVEMENT AND TRAVEL

INTRODUCTION

The ability to move knowledgeably, confidently, safely, and independently through the environment is perhaps the most important skill the blind/VI child must gain. This is truly a foundational skill, forming the basis for many aspects of future autonomy and independence in life. This is the skill that enables a child to walk over to a friend's house, cross streets safely, go to a neighborhood store, negotiate hallways in a busy school building, participate in gym class, handle the lunch line, find a seat in a crowded room, play in the playground, manage school trips, and eventually navigate a college campus, get to work, and travel freely—all with confidence, grace, and independence. Independent movement and travel is not a curriculum or lesson or class—it is a foundation for most aspects of life.

Independent movement and travel is often referred to as Orientation and Mobility, or O&M. *Orientation* means knowing where you are in relation to other objects, places, and people in the environment. *Mobility* refers to the ability to get where you want to go.

Getting Ready for College Begins in Third Grade: Working Toward an Independent Future for Your Blind/Visually Impaired Child, pp. 39–67
Copyright © 2010 by Information Age Publishing
All rights of reproduction in any form reserved.

EXPECTATIONS

As with so many other aspects of bringing up a blind/VI child, this one starts with attitudes and expectations. First, parents need to become educated and raise their own awareness and expectations. For example, do you know that a blind woman raced twice in the 1150-mile Iditarod dog sled race? That a blind man sailed solo from San Francisco to Hawaii? That a blind guy climbed Mount Everest? That blind people run marathons? That blind people use the New York City subway system every day to get to school and work? Once parents have a new picture in their minds of what is possible for a blind/VI person, they'll be much more able to raise their child with age-appropriate expectations for movement and independence. All that's left to learn after that is how to do it!

At first, informed parents may be the only ones who have these higher expectations. Others in the family, on the school team, or in the community may assume that the child's potential for independent movement and travel is very limited. Parents often find themselves in the role of teacher and role model, enabling others to see their blind/VI child taking a walk, going to the store, participating in dance class, climbing on playground equipment, and, in general, enjoying a normal life.

The goal is for the child to grow up to be an independent adult who is able to move about confidently, competently, and independently and go where he/she wants to go. Parents who learn from blind/VI adults and the field of O&M to hold normal expectations at each stage of development—and then add love, devotion, time, and determination—will make sure their child is on the road to independent movement and travel.

WHAT WE ARE AIMING FOR

The competent blind/VI adult traveler is gathering information through the senses, using good cane skills, and drawing on the store of knowledge collected over years of experience to figure out the environment and make good movement and travel decisions. Contrary to popular belief, blind/VI people are not out in the world without a clue. Rather, they have a great deal of information and many skills at their disposal, especially if they have received good training and have had the opportunity to practice. Among the many skills the good blind/VI traveler uses are hearing, information received through the cane and through the feet, memory, spatial understanding, mental mapping, residual vision, sense of smell, and the ability to ask good questions to gain additional information when needed. As travel instructor Doug Boone puts it, "Your cane and your brain—don't leave home without them!" (personal communication, April 20, 1999).

Becoming a Competent Traveler: It's a Process

Your child's development toward independent movement and travel is a process. Naturally, he or she will not have all the skills and experience necessary to be safe in all situations at first. But in order to develop the skills, the child needs opportunities to encounter and learn about the structures in the physical world and to learn and practice movement skills in real-life situations. So, while you will of course be watching over your young blind/VI child, as you would any other young child, do so in a way that enables the child to move independently, encounter and explore, and gain firsthand experience with the world. Provide opportunities for your child to practice the skills he/she is learning. As you observe your child moving, you will identify areas that require additional teaching. In the meantime, your child is getting practice in moving in the world. With practice comes increasing skill and, finally, mastery.

A Developmental Process

The formal field of Orientation and Mobility (O&M) came into existence after World War II to serve blinded veterans. Because they were formerly sighted, the veterans already had the concepts and skills needed for safe travel as sighted people—they knew about distance, intersections, traffic flow, stop signs, and traffic lights. They knew how to take buses and trains, navigate sidewalks, and cross streets. What they had to learn were the new techniques that would enable them to do these same things without eyesight.

For young blind/VI children, however, it is a different story. The process is developmental. Children do not start by learning formal techniques. They start by experiencing the world, making contact with objects and structures in the environment, and building basic concepts that will eventually enable them to construct a mental picture of their environment. Later, they learn formal techniques.

MOVEMENT IS KEY

Get your child moving! Movement brings the child into contact with the objects, people, and places in the environment. This contact leads to discovery, curiosity, and exploration and lays the foundation for the development of concepts, comprehension, and problem-solving. It also begins the development of a store of knowledge about objects and places that your child will use later in independent travel.

Figure 4.1.   Discovery learning—a child explores a fountain.

Moving also enables your child to discover what his/her own body can do. In order to be a full participant in life, your child needs to develop the same repertoire of independent movement skills that other children have—walking, running, jumping, balancing, twisting, turning, kicking, climbing, et cetera. Let your child move under his/her own steam! Are you carrying your sweet, cuddly blind/VI child beyond the age that sighted children are being carried? Put her down! Do you always hold hands with your child? Let go! Are you lifting your little guy into the car seat when he could learn to climb in himself? Teach him to climb in!

Moving about and coming into contact with objects and places in the environment also establishes the beginnings of spatial awareness and mental mapping. Through movement, your child will begin to make connections between different parts of a room and different rooms in your home. Later on, this ability will enable him/her to create mental maps of larger indoor spaces, unfamiliar spaces, and outdoor spaces.

Last but not least, moving under his/her own power, discovering and exploring objects and places, and finding out how his/her body can move mean that the child is becoming an active participant in the world and living life in the mainstream. Blind/VI children are very vulnerable to being

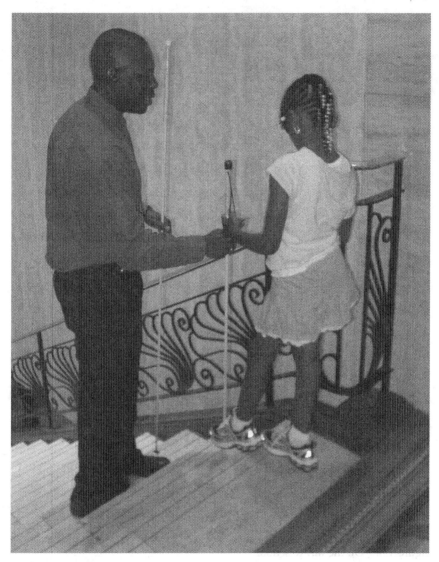

Figure 4.2. A mobility lesson in progress.

acted upon—people are always bringing things *to* them, perhaps afraid that if they go to get something, they might trip or make a mess. When they are walking, people are likely to guide them, pulling or pushing them along, turning them, "steering" them around by the shoulders. Too many of these experiences could teach a child to be passive or to bristle under the constant touch of others and become uncooperative.

Figure 4.3.   On the way to school.

Instead, we want the child to enjoy moving, to become capable in physical movements, and to view him/herself as an active, effective person in the world. We want the child to become a doer, not a done-to-er.

Sometimes parents (and others) are afraid to let the child move independently—but please remember that without lots of independent movement experiences, the child cannot develop the spatial awareness, motor

Figure 4.4.   Running a good race.

skills, concepts, and understanding that lead to independent mobility and good travel decisions. Early movement experiences lead to learning the way to school, dragging out the garbage cans, participating in athletics,

Figure 4.5.   Enjoying a hair-raising gymnastics class.

Figure 4.6.   A blind/VI child benefits from a variety of independent movement experiences.

living away at college, getting to work, pulling a baby stroller, and having a full, satisfying, independent life.

Encouraging Movement in the Home

In the early years, parents can create a stimulating environment at home, one that encourages the child to move from place to place in order to find all the interesting things there are to do. For example, the child might discover that the music player is in the dining room, there are pots and pans to bang on in the kitchen, and the trampoline is in the family room. Provide opportunities throughout the house for your child to learn that his/her movements and actions can make things happen and have an effect.

Let the child fully explore the kitchen, the basement, the garage, the shed. Encourage all the "how" questions: How does an omelet get made? Let the child get out the eggs and the frying pan. How does the vacuum cleaner actually pick up the dirt? Let him or her follow the length of the hose, feel the suction, and experiment with what the vacuum can and cannot pick up. How do the garbage cans get out to the curb every few days?

And, speaking of garbage cans, household tasks are a great way to develop movement skills. Assign your blind/VI child chores and household tasks, just as you would a sighted child. If you don't know how a blind/VI person would accomplish the task safely and efficiently, call a blind/VI friend, read back issues of the *Braille Monitor* and *Future Reflections* magazines, ask a teacher of the blind/VI, or contact members of the National Federation of the Blind. They will be glad to help.

DEVELOPING SPATIAL AWARENESS

Spatial awareness means understanding the position of objects in the environment, understanding where you are in relation to other people and objects in the environment, and understanding your body's position in that space. It is crucial for blind/VI children to develop this understanding if they are to become competent, efficient, independent travelers.

You can work on these concepts both as specific lessons and as they come up in daily life. Below are some areas to pay attention to:

Body Awareness

- Names of body parts
- Front/back/side of body
- Right/left of child's own body
- Right/left of someone else's body when facing the child; when standing in front of the child but facing away from child

Tip for Teaching Right and Left

For a child having difficulty remembering which is right and which is left, try this method (Sadako Vargas, personal communication). Refer to the "right side" and the "other side" (leaving out the word *left* for the time being). Whenever it's time to turn right, say "We've got to make a RIGHT turn," putting emphasis on the word *right* while taking two fingers and moving them across the child's back along the shoulders from the left to the right, and then pulling the child's right arm out to the side so the child's arm is "pointing" to the right. You will be getting the feel of "rightness" into the child's body. The child may then be better able to remember which is the right side and which is the "other" side. When you feel confident that your child knows which one is the right side, you can begin using the word *left*.

Comparison Words

- Small/smaller/smallest
- Big/bigger/biggest
- Short/shorter/shortest
- Long/longer/longest

Shapes and Shape Words

- Circle, square, rectangle, triangle, round, rectangular, triangular, straight, curved, et cetera.

Position Words

- In front of
- Behind/In back of
- Next to/Beside
- On top of
- Underneath/Below

Other Words Indicating Order and Position

- First, second, third
- Next, last, next to last
- Closer, farther, et cetera. For example, "Put the bigger rock closer to you and the smaller one farther away," or, "Line up all the shape pieces—put the circle first, then the square, and then the triangle third."

Sound Location

Give your child practice locating where a sound is coming from. Have him/her point to the sound, move to the source of the sound, and use directional words to describe where the sound is coming from (for example, "up ahead on the right" or "behind me on the left").

Echolocation

Echolocation is the ability to use the presence or absence of reflected sound to locate objects in the environment before actually touching them.

For example, a blind/VI person using this ability can walk down a street and sense the presence of a car parked on the sidewalk in front of him and negotiate around it without running into it. Another extremely useful way this ability can be used is to listen for open doors along a hallway or for an intersecting hallway.

Once children become aware of this phenomenon, they can use it for all kinds of exploration and travel tasks. To learn more about developing this and other movement abilities in children, please see *Independent Movement and Travel in Blind Children: A Promotion Model* by Joe Cutter.

Making 90° Turns

Ninety-degree turns are the most common turns your child will need to make when moving about in the environment. For helping the child get the feeling of 90° turns, have the child stand in a corner with his/her back against one wall and side against the other. Have him turn right or left and notice which parts of his body are now touching the walls. This can help the child understand the concept.

Clock Positions

Although fewer and fewer people tell time using a clock face, for travel purposes, it is useful for a blind/VI child to learn how to use clock positions as an adjunct to using degrees for turns (90°, 45°, etc.). Have the child imagine that 12 o'clock is directly in front and 6 o'clock directly in back. You can then tell the child to "head toward 1 o'clock" or "the car is just about at 11 o'clock."

Cardinal Directions

- North, east, south, west, northeast, southeast, northwest, southwest

Geometric Terms

- Horizontal, vertical, parallel, perpendicular, diagonal, across

Directions to Locations

Give your child practice following directions both inside the house and out. For example, at home, ask him/her to get something for you in a pantry or on a closet shelf: "The crayons are in the closet in a square plastic box on a shelf about waist-high all the way on the right." At the library, say, "To get to the Children's Room, we need to go down the stairs, turn left, and then look for the second room on the right. Can you get us there?"

Practice like this, along with the development of the other skills listed in this chapter, will eventually enable your child to follow street directions to outside destinations.

Maps

Experience with maps, globes, and map concepts will help your child develop spatial awareness. You can even "draw" simple maps on your child's back with your finger, which can enable him/her to internalize some of these concepts (Sadako Vargas, personal communication). For example: "The room is square" ("draw" a square on the child's back with your finger). "We're standing here" (make an X to indicate the place), "and we need to get to the snack table, which is up in this corner" (run your finger up toward the destination and draw another X). "We need to go straight across the room and then turn right to get to the table" (move your finger up and to the right as you say the words).

Another way to develop spatial concepts is to play a game in which the child sits on the edge of a foam mat about 3' by 4' in size (Sadako Vargas, personal communication). Put a smaller mat in front of the child and place a doll or figure on the edge of the small mat in the same position as the child.

Have the child crawl along one edge of the larger mat to a corner and then turn and crawl to the next corner. The child then returns to the starting position and moves the doll through the same path along the doll's mat. You can also have the child move the doll around the small mat first and then move him/herself in the same way along the larger mat.

Another idea is for your child to create maps of familiar places (for example, your kitchen or a familiar route) using Wikki Stix (see page 60).

DEVELOPING THE STORE OF KNOWLEDGE: GOING PLACES

Take your child to lots of places—he/she needs firsthand experience with the supermarket, the post office, the bank, the mall, the fire house, the movie theater, the park, a farm, town hall, a hotel, stairwells, elevators, escalators, et cetera. The information your child gains from these first-hand experiences will enable him/her to know about everything that

Table 4.1.   Developing the Store of Knowledge

Does your child know what he/she can expect to see or find...

In a classroom	In a sports arena
In a school hallway	In a movie theater
At the library	In a concert hall
In a post office	In a hotel lobby
At an business office	At a corner
In a doctor's office	Along a city street
In a waiting room	Along a country road
In a public restroom	At a bus stop
At a small store	In a train station
In a supermarket	In an airport
In a big box store	At a gas station
In a mall	In a garage

sighted children know about. Even more importantly for mobility purposes, this information will form the knowledge base that your child will use for future independent mobility. This store of knowledge will enable your child to know what is likely to be found in a variety of settings, to figure things out, and to make good movement decisions. Some of this information can be gained by reading or hearing about various places, but it is direct experience that will enable your child to perceive and comprehend the information on his/her own and translate that into safe, sound movement decisions.

GUIDED DISCOVERY

Another goal as you visit various places is for your child to learn *how to explore and how to gain useful information from the exploration.* Parents can train their blind/VI children in this very important skill by using the guided discovery method. Guided discovery teaches the child how to get information him/herself and how to begin making connections between new information and information already known. Guided discovery launches the child into learning the methods that he/she will really use in the future.

A major technique of the guided discovery method is asking "leading questions" that guide the child toward exploring in a fruitful way, extracting useful information and drawing logical conclusions. Please note: *The parent does not provide the information. He/she asks the questions that will enable the child to figure out the information.*

Here are some examples of how this might look:

Parent and child are walking toward the corner in a familiar neighborhood. The child stops.

Parent: Why did you stop?
Child: I thought we were there.
Parent: Why did you think that?
Child: I felt a slope down.
Parent: So what might that be?
Child: The curb cut?
Parent: Is there anything else it might be?
Child: A driveway.
Parent: Is there any way you can tell the difference?
Child: [No answer]
Parent: Is there any way you can tell if you are at the corner?
Child: I can listen to the traffic?
Parent: So what do you think?
Child: I can hear it.
Parent: So how can that help you know if you're at the corner?
Child: How close it sounds.
Parent: Good. So what do you think?
Child: It's still a little far away.
Parent: So what do you think we should do?
Child: Walk a little more.

They walk on. Child stops again.

Parent: Why did you stop now?
Child: I think this is the curb cut.
Parent: Anything else?
Child: I hear the cars in front of us.
Parent: Are they very close?
Child: Yes.
Parent: Is there anything else you know about this corner?
Child: It has a fire hydrant.
Parent: So what do you think?
Child: I could look for the hydrant.
Parent: Okay.

Child searches with cane for the hydrant.

Parent: So what do you think?
Child: We're at the corner.

* * *

Parent and child are walking to a familiar store. Child stops.

Parent: Why did you stop?
Child: [No answer]
Parent: What are we looking for?
Child: [No answer]
Parent: Do you know anything about the store we are going to?
Child: It has plastic chairs out front.
Parent: Anything else?
Child: A big flower pot.
Parent: So what do you think?
Child: My cane touched something.
Parent: What might that be?
Child: The flower pot?
Parent: Okay. Is there any way you could double check?
Child: I could look for the chairs.
Parent: Good.

Child looks for the chairs.

Parent: So what do you think?
Child: This is the right store.

After hearing you ask this type of question many, many times, two things will happen: First, the child will begin to be able to ask him/herself the questions and will have learned how to get information independently. Second, your child will be creating a real store of knowledge based on information he/she experienced firsthand, knowledge that will enable him/her in future independent travel to successfully problem-solve and figure things out.

The Role of Verbal Description

But what about verbal description, you might ask. While there certainly is a place for verbal description, there really is no substitute for the child, especially the young child, experiencing things firsthand and learning how to gather information for him/herself. You, the sighted parent, may gain virtually all your information through your eyesight. However, filling your blind/VI child up with information *you* gained through full eyesight will not teach your child how to gain information for him/herself through the channels he/she has available, especially for future travel purposes.

If you truly are envisioning an independent future for your child, make sure you give him/her opportunities to gain the information independently. Resist providing a constant stream of verbal information! Find a good balance between discovery and description. Perhaps a good rule of thumb would be that if the child can find the information out independently, let him/her. Initially, your words can help make connections and fill in blanks, but remember that the goal is for the child to learn to do this him/herself. Verbal description can be a useful adjunct for discovery, but not a substitute for it.

The Role of *Sighted Guide*

This mobility technique, also known as *human guide*, is typically the first technique taught in conventional O&M lessons, even before the use of the cane. For newly blinded adults, it might make sense to teach this technique first, to ease the transition to functioning without eyesight. For blind/VI children, however, the situation is completely different.

Unlike newly blinded adults, most young blind/VI children do not need to get used to being blind/VI; they need to get used to moving independently. So, for blind/VI children, the emphasis from the start must be on *independent* movement:

- The child must get used to the feeling of moving under his/her own power.
- The child must learn to make his/her own movement decisions.

Neither of these will occur if the child is always guided.

Unfortunately, because it is traditional to teach "sighted guide" before teaching the use of a cane, most photos illustrating the technique show the blind/VI person walking without using his/her cane. This is not good! Your child should *always* be using his/her cane to get direct information about what is underfoot and what is ahead—including when holding the arm of another person.

It is only through experience and the chance to practice moving independently that your child will become an efficient traveler and an effective monitor of his or her own safety. Handing over the responsibility for movement decisions and safety to a sighted person seems to be rooted in old-fashioned thinking, in which a blind/VI person is considered helpless and is expected to learn to "trust" all the nice sighted people who will be providing help. In fact, even the assumption that the guide will be the sighted person is a poor one. There are many times when the blind/VI person has the information about where to go and is giving the directions. A better term for the technique is *paired walking*.

There are other problems with the sighted guide technique. Whole chapters of books are devoted to teaching it, although it is really quite simple and only requires common sense to employ. The time spent focusing on sighted guide would be much better spent giving the child practice using a cane and moving independently.

Another problem is that when instructors teach this technique to the adults in the blind/VI child's life, it can actually become a real barrier to true independent movement and travel. *It is very easy for this technique to be overused.* School personnel love it because they believe it will keep their student safe. They also see it as an easy, efficient way to get the child from point A to point B. After all, giving the child opportunities to move on his/her own and to problem-solve takes time. Parents also like it because it seems to make life easier. But realize this: It may take less time; it may be convenient and less trouble in the short run—but *it does not lead to independent movement and travel.*

Think about the future. While there are times when using this technique might be appropriate—such as when you are trying to stay together in a crowd—use it sparingly, at most, and always in combination with your child's cane.

ENVIRONMENTAL INFORMATION

Even when your child is quite young, you can start building awareness of the wealth of environmental information available. These are the clues that your child will use later in independent mobility. When you are out taking a walk together, bring your child's attention to the sounds, smells, and other sensations that can be perceived in both the natural and the human-made environment—the feeling of the sun on your faces, the smell of pines, the hum of a generator, the hissing sound from inside the dry cleaner, the bell at a gas station, the aroma of the donut shop. You can begin this kind of training when your little one is still in a stroller or baby pack! Start your child early with paying attention to the environment and it will soon become automatic.

Here are some ideas:

- Sounds in the environment: Construction sounds, a lawn mower, a radio playing
- Voices: Children laughing ("Oh, we must be near the park!"); a group of people talking ("I hear lots of voices ahead of us. We'd better move to the side so that we don't bump into them.")

- The sound of traffic moving, starting, and stopping ("That traffic is passing right in front of our noses. We'd better stop!" "Now I hear the traffic going past me on the right.")
- The feeling and sound underfoot and under cane: What kind of surface are you walking on—grass, pavement, sidewalk, brick, dirt, gravel?
- Sidewalks—how they run and what might be found on them ("Whoa, what did your cane find?"—bikes, toys, garbage and recycling cans, newspapers)
- The grass on lawns and near the street
- Driveways, curbs, and curb cuts ("Oh, I feel my feet going up/down a little. I wonder if this is the curb cut at the corner. Yes, I hear the sound of cars very near. We must be at the corner.") Your child needs more than just the information underfoot to understand what curb cuts and driveways are like. Let him/her crawl around on them and examine them to really find out what the slope looks like and what causes the feelings underfoot.
- How the street slopes up and then down again as you cross
- How long does it take to cross the street?
- What is a block? How far is a block? How long does it take to walk it?
- What is a square block?
- How long is a quarter-mile? How much time does it take to walk it?
- What street are we walking along? What street are we headed toward?
- The line of buildings on your town's main street—listen to them, reach out and touch them
- Alleyways between buildings
- The newspaper bin and mailbox on the corner, a fire hydrant, street sign, stop sign, lamp post, telephone pole, storm drain—all of these can be eventual landmarks for your child and will add to his/her store of knowledge about what might be found at corners.
- Trees, bushes, hedges, fences, walls—more potential landmarks

If your child gets into the habit of paying attention to things in the environment, he/she will be well prepared for the more complex mobility tasks that lie ahead.

O&M CONCEPTS

When it comes time for your child to venture down the block alone or to learn to cross the street, you and the mobility instructor will talk about many orientation and mobility concepts. Go along on lessons if you can so that you can understand the goals, teaching methods, and mobility techniques your child will be learning. You can then provide follow-up practice between lessons.

Your child will be learning about many things:

- Traffic sounds and traffic patterns—stop streets, lighted and unlighted intersections
- Types of intersections (plus, T, Y) and street layouts
- Parallel traffic; perpendicular traffic
- Making good turns
- Making a straight crossing versus veering
- Cardinal directions: north, east, south, west, northeast, southwest, et cetera
- The sun's movement over time
- The time–distance connection
- Maps
- Compasses
- How to learn a new place
- How to take mobility notes

Ideas for Teaching Concepts

Some basic, essential concepts can be difficult to understand fully if they cannot be seen or touched in their entirety, for example, a square block or an intersection. The mobility instructor can provide map kits that can help, but if your child needs additional ways to access these concepts, here are some ideas:

- Many children seem better able to learn a concept when it is demonstrated on their own body first. For example, to demonstrate the relationship of two sides of a street, have the child sit in a chair with legs next to each other. "Here are the two sides of Maple Avenue." (Have the child run his/her hands up and down his/her legs.) "We live on the east side of Maple." (Touch the right leg.) "Grandma lives across the street on the west side of Maple." (Touch the left leg.) In order to get to her house, we have to go across the street." (The child's hand goes from one leg across to the other.)
- Use a square or rectangular table to work on the idea of a square block. Mark a point on the edge of the table with something that the child can easily find as a starting and ending place. Have the

child touch the table with his/her body and/or hand as he/she goes around.

- o "Now we're walking along Central Avenue. This is block number one. Oh, we've reached a corner—we have to turn. Let's go left. Now we're walking along Main Street. This is block number two. It's a longer block than Central Avenue, isn't it? Here's the next corner. Let's go left again. Now we're walking along Maple Avenue. This is block number three. Here's the corner. Let's go left again. This is block number four. Now we're on Walnut Street. Here's the corner. Let's go left one more time. Hmmm, I wonder what street we're on now. Any ideas? Look, we've come back to where we started. So we got back to Central Avenue."

- o You can then work on relating the walk around the table to a "walk" around a square block on a tactile map. Then go out and take a real walk around the block.

- For building an understanding of streets and directions, lie down on the floor and have your child sit or kneel next to you. Stretch your arms out along the floor above your head. Place an item on the floor just beyond your fingertips to represent the North Pole.

- o Tell your child, "I am Main Street. My feet are the south end of Main Street. My fingertips are the north end." Have the child feel along your body to the "south" and to the "north." Then tell the child, "Go down to my feet [the child will be on all fours] and 'walk' along me toward my head and fingertips. [Child should be crawling alongside you, touching you.] You are 'walking' north along Main Street! Can you find the North Pole?"

- o "Okay, time to cross the street." Child climbs/crawls over you. "Okay, make a left turn and now head south on Main Street."

- When you are out walking, practice using phrases such as, "We are walking along Oak Avenue heading toward Birch Street"; "Now we're at the corner of Oak and Birch. We have three choices—we can go straight, right, or left."

- Do a lot of listening at corners before crossing the street. Point out the sound of the perpendicular or intersecting traffic crossing in front of your noses. If there is parallel traffic—going past your shoulders on the right or left—talk to your child about making a safe crossing and not veering toward the sound of that passing traffic.

- If your child is having difficulty understanding how to use a map, have him/her make one him/herself of a very familiar area, for example, your own street and the next intersecting street. Get some Wikki Stix and tell your child to "draw" your street (child lays down a strand of Wikki Stix). Then say, "Let's go out of our house and turn right and walk along our street" (child moves his/her hand or finger along the "street"). "Ah, we've reached the corner. What street is at the end of our block? Yes, Dogwood Lane. Okay, can you "draw" Dogwood Lane?" (Child lays another piece of Wikki Stix perpendicular to the first one.) Continue to add "streets" as your child is able. You can then practice routes to various places along the streets.

DOES MY CHILD NEED A CANE?

Although parents often feel relieved when they hear that their partially sighted child does not "need" a cane, they often still wonder if their youngster would benefit from using one. One way to decide is to determine whether or not the child has the freedom and ability to move around in the environment with as much safety and confidence as fully sighted children of the same age. For example, on a school trip, does someone always have to stay with the child and hold her hand or warn her if there are steps down? Is the child able to easily discern when there is a drop-off such as a curb, or does he have to slow down, move very cautiously, and feel with his foot? If sighted children of the same age are crossing quiet streets independently, is the partially sighted child able to do that, too? Or does she need to be watched, verbally directed, or held onto? All these indicate that the child would be safer, more efficient, and more independent with a cane in hand.

Things to Watch For

Here are a few ways to determine whether or not a cane would enable your child to move faster, more independently, more confidently, and in a more relaxed manner.

- Do you find yourself providing a constant stream of verbal directions? "Watch out, there's a bicycle on the sidewalk"; "Be careful, there's a tree root just ahead"; "Slow down, there's a step down in front of you."

- Do you find yourself moving your child to the right or left or "steering" him/her around by the shoulders?

- Does your child always want to or *need* to hold your hand (especially beyond the age when this is usually done)?

- Is someone always monitoring the child's movement (past the age where this would be done for a fully sighted child)?

- Does your child use his/her foot as a feeler? Some blind/VI adults walk with their feet "toes out," forming a V, the result of not having a cane, yet trying to gain a little more information through the feet. See if your child is getting in to this habit.

- Is your child relaxed and confident in new environments? In bright sunlight? When it is dark?

The Bottom Line

If someone else is monitoring a child's movement, that child is not learning to do it him/herself. If someone else is making judgments about when it is safe to go and when it is not, the child is not learning how to do it him/herself. If someone is guiding the child around either verbally or physically, the child will get used to it and will learn to be dependent on someone else's movement decisions. If someone is always guiding your child around obstacles, then your child is not learning how to detect, identify, and navigate around them him/herself. If someone else is filling your child up with information gained visually, your child will not learn how to gain environmental information him/herself.

The only way to develop the ability and judgment to navigate the environment safely, skillfully, and knowledgeably is for the child to do it him/herself. The partially sighted child who "uses eyesight for what he can see and the cane for what he can't see" will become a relaxed, confident, graceful, speedy, successful independent traveler.

Is My Child Ready for a Cane?

In the past, children were given canes only when they were deemed to be ready for formal cane techniques, that is, when they had the muscle control to hold their hand and arm in a certain position and to coordinate the movements of arm and legs. This was usually at about fifteen years old. These days, kids are given canes as soon as they can stand up and sometimes even before!

Very young children should not be expected to use the cane with adult technique. Instead, they will use the cane in a manner consistent with their developmental stage. The important thing is to make sure your child is not denied a cane because "he/she is not ready." (For a full discussion of the cane as a developmental tool, see *Independent Movement and Travel in Blind Children: A Promotion Model*, 2007, by Joe Cutter.)

Cane Travel Basics

The cane is held so that the tip lands two or three steps in front of the feet. It is swept from side to side just slightly wider than shoulder width. Like vision, the cane gives a preview of what lies ahead and to the sides. It tells if a path is clear or if an object is in the way and locates a safe spot to place the foot. It alerts the user to drop-offs like curbs and enables safe negotiation of stairs up or down. As the user moves along, the cane touches various things, enabling the user to identify objects and to contact or avoid them as desired.

Characteristics of Canes

Several types of canes are available: metal, fiberglass, carbon fiber, rigid, folding, telescoping. For the young child who is still developing motor skills, strength, and dexterity, a *longer, lightweight, rigid* cane with *a narrow grip* and *metal tip* often works best to promote confident, comfortable independent movement and exploration of the environment.

- The young child usually cannot yet hold the cane in a centered position in front of his/her body and might hold it resting against the hip. A longer cane (up to the child's chin or nose) can make up for this lack of motor skill.
- The longer length also gives an extra step before the child's body will come into contact with an object the cane has struck, giving the child more reaction time.
- A lighter cane material (such as fiberglass) allows the cane to be a little longer but still lightweight. A lightweight cane is more maneuverable and less tiring for a child to hold.
- A rigid lightweight cane (as opposed to a folding or telescoping cane) conveys good feedback/information to the child's hand and

arm. It also enables the child to handle the cane independently (not needing an adult to help unfold it, etc.).

- A narrow grip (as opposed to a golf grip) is comfortable to hold for long periods of time, thereby encouraging the young child to keep the cane in his/her hand.

- A metal tip provides excellent echo and sound information when the child taps the cane or when the cane strikes an object, wall, or door. A "marshmallow" tip or ball tip tends to roll right over information without conveying it through to the arm. With less environmental information, the child will be less equipped to make good movement decisions.

As the child continues in the developmental process and gains more and more motor control, he/she will begin to hold the cane with a more standard grip and position. Eventually, the child will hold the cane with the hand centered, sliding or tapping it with a low arc from side to side, and walking "in step," with the cane tip to the right when the left foot is forward and the cane tip to the left when the right foot is forward. Learning and mastering these techniques enable the child to keep him/herself safe while walking briskly, purposefully, and gracefully from place to place.

Sleepshades

For partially sighted children, sleepshades (blindfolds) are often used during cane lessons. The idea is for the child to concentrate on the information coming in through the cane without being distracted by visual input. The child learns that he/she can rely on the information received through the cane and the other senses to make good movement decisions and becomes more confident in his/her movement. As the child progresses and integrates eyesight back in, he/she learns when his/her sight is reliable and when it is not. Because he/she has fully learned to use the cane nonvisually, the child will be able to move safely and independently even under lighting conditions that previously might have been difficult, such as darkness, glare, or bright sunshine.

Teaching Cane

The idea of using a teaching cane occurred to early childhood mobility specialist Joe Cutter when he observed blind/VI students learning cane travel from blind/VI instructors who were also using canes (personal comunication). Joe noticed how natural it was for the students to pay attention to and learn from the sounds of the instructor's cane as it was tapped and swept from side to side. He began using a teaching cane himself and dispensing teaching canes to parents and teachers who would be following up on cane lessons. A teaching cane serves many purposes, from providing a positive example, to giving sound feedback to the child, to building an understanding for the sighted adults in the child's life of how the cane works. A teaching cane can be a very effective tool to use as your child learns to travel with a cane.

CONSIDERATIONS FOR SCHOOL

The mobility goal for school is for the child to move about the school environment with age-appropriate independence and autonomy. To achieve this goal, several components must be in place for both the student and school personnel.

Student Training

Your child will probably receive lessons from an O&M instructor. Find out the goals the instructor has in mind for your child and, if possible, go along on a few lessons so that you can see what your child is learning and provide follow-up at home. If there is a classroom aide in the picture, he/she should go along to lessons as well, again, to learn what the child is learning in order to provide practice and follow-up between lessons and to facilitate your child's growing independence.

Exploration

The young child—or the older child who has not had this opportunity in the past—needs ample time to explore the classroom, the hallways, the cafeteria, the library, the gym, the restrooms, the playground. Becoming familiar with these areas will enable the child to self-orient and get around independently. In addition, this exploration will contribute to the child's store of knowledge about what can be found in a school environment.

Time for Problem-Solving

For the young child, an extremely important component of the development of independent movement and travel skills is time for problem-solving. Whenever possible, the child should have the opportunity to make guided discoveries about the school environment and guided decisions about which way to move. If movement decisions are always made *for* the child, when will the child learn to make them independently? If a constant stream of verbal instructions is provided or if the child is always being physically led or guided, when will he or she learn to find places and handle stairs or obstacles in the environment him/herself?

Teacher Education

In order to achieve the goal of age-appropriate independence and autonomy in the school environment, it will probably be necessary to raise the awareness of classroom teachers and other school staff. It is likely that school personnel will initially be very concerned about your child's safety when he/she is moving about the building. They will probably not know about the information, tools, and techniques that blind/VI people use to travel about safely and independently. They might be imagining how difficult it must be to go up and down stairs, find a classroom, or maneuver in the cafeteria without sight. So it is essential for teachers to become aware that blind/VI people travel safely, efficiently, and independently every day. Tell them about the blind man who scaled Mt. Everest! Let them know that blind people travel through airports, use subways, and navigate busy city streets. This awareness will raise their expectations, hopefully allay their fears about your child's independent mobility, and keep them from being overprotective.

Next, your child will make the most progress if teachers become generally familiar with the skills he/she is learning and using. For example, if teachers understand how a cane is used, they will respect and encourage its use. If they understand the need for problem-solving, they will build in time for this whenever possible. As mentioned earlier, if there is a classroom aide, he/she can learn and then provide practice and follow-up between mobility lessons.

Remember, the development of independent travel skills is a process, and the more that teachers learn about the process, the faster your child will progress. If given appropriate training and opportunity to practice and problem solve, the blind/VI student, as the months go on, becomes increasingly skilled, increasingly independent, and increasingly able to take responsibility for his/her own safety. As the student develops skills, the amount of protection (and concern) should diminish. It won't happen in a day; but if it isn't planned for, it won't happen at all!

Promoting Age-Appropriate Independence and Autonomy

With a little effort, the school team can create an atmosphere through-out the school that encourages age-appropriate independence and auton-omy. When expectations for independent functioning are in place, along with an understanding of the progression of independent mobility skills, progress will occur.

Make sure the child is perceived as capable and able to do things for him/herself. If the child needs more training, make sure he/she gets it. Teach the teachers not to help too much. If others view the child as help-less, the child soon will view him/herself that way, too. Set up the child's desk area for independent functioning. Make sure others are not always getting things for the child. The child should be learning the skills that enable him/her to move about the classroom and other areas of the school—hallways, stairways, restrooms, lunchroom, gym, library, play-ground—with the same freedom and ability as sighted peers.

While concern for the safety of all students is appropriate, the key for the blind/VI child is to keep the concern from turning into overprotec-tion. Make sure school personnel do not restrict the child's movement based on their fears or their *assumptions* about what would or would not be safe. Instead, make sure the child learns the skills to keep him/herself safe. Hovering over the child and overprotection will not allow this pro-cess to occur.

Make sure the child is allowed to walk under his/her own power and is not always guided or "steered" (this includes constant verbal guidance). Make sure he/she develops the skills to walk in line with classmates and is not always put at the beginning or the end of the line. Avoid sighted guide and holding hands with the child long after what would be considered age-appropriate. Familiarize the child with stairway doors and exit doors. Make sure the child uses the cane for fire drills so that in the case of a real emergency, he/she has a way to exit the school building independently if necessary.

Don't let your child be held back by other people's negative attitudes, low expectations, and inappropriate actions. Instead, invite teachers to be on the team that has as its goal a child who is competent, independent, autonomous, self-motivated, self-directed, and responsible in all move-ment areas.

RECOMMENDED BOOKS

In view of the serious shortage of O&M instructors, many parents are searching for ways in which they can enhance their child's independent movement. The following books are excellent sources of information, lesson plans, et cetera. All are available at www.nfb.org.

- *Independent Movement and Travel in Blind Children: A Promotion Model* (2007) by Joe Cutter;
- *Modular Instruction for Independent Travel for Students Who Are Blind or Visually Impaired: Preschool through High School* (1998) by Doris Willoughby and Sharon Monthei;
- *Techniques Used by Blind Cane Travel Instructors—A Practical Approach* (1997) by Maria Morais et al.; and
- *The Care and Feeding of the Long White Cane: Instructions in Cane Travel for Blind People* (1993) by Thomas Bickford.

YOUR INDEPENDENT TRAVELER

The child who has had many experiences, who has built up a good store of knowledge, who has had opportunities to practice and develop independent movement skills, and who has been encouraged to take the normal steps toward age-appropriate independence and self-responsibility will be a child ready to meet the challenges of the larger middle school or high school environment and will be able to look toward the future with competence and confidence.

CHAPTER 5

SOCIAL AWARENESS
AND SOCIAL SKILLS

INTRODUCTION

It's often said that success in life doesn't come from brains alone. Personality and the ability to interact with people count just as much, if not more. Think about the future and the social interaction skills your child will need at college or at work: walking into a room and meeting a stranger who will become a roommate, living with another person, making new friends, being a friend without being a burden, having dinner conversation, discussing blindness/visual impairment with a professor, making testing arrangements with a professor, hiring and working with readers, going to a dance, going on a date, joining a club or organization, doing community service, going on a job interview, discussing work responsibilities, being friendly at a new worksite, having lunch with a group. If you want your child to have success in later life, working on social skills now is a smart idea.

THE DEVELOPMENT OF SOCIAL SKILLS

For many children, blind and sighted alike, the development of social skills is natural and comes easily. They just "pick them up" through their

Getting Ready for College Begins in Third Grade: Working Toward an Independent Future for Your Blind/Visually Impaired Child, pp. 69–86
Copyright © 2010 by Information Age Publishing

own instincts and observations. If your child is one of these, you probably don't even need to read this chapter. But if you have a child for whom these skills are not coming naturally, then the information contained here will be helpful.

The development of social skills can be challenging for children with disabilities for a variety of reasons. For some children, the majority of their time in the early years is spent going to medical appointments and therapies. They end up interacting much more with adults—doctors, therapists, early intervention specialists, teachers—than with their own peers. They therefore don't get the same experience and opportunity to develop and practice social skills as other children their age. While other kids are learning how to share and take turns, the blind/VI child might be getting very good at balancing on a therapy ball or responding to a thera-pist's requests. The lack of opportunity and experience can even lead to a lack of interest in playing with other children. Other children do possess the social skills but might face the bias that is still present in our society against people who are different in some way.

If you have a child who is experiencing difficulties in this area, there is good news—there are many ways in which parents can intervene and help social development take place, and, as your child sees how the new skills are of benefit, he/she will be motivated to keep progressing. Let's start with exactly what is expected of us in social situations. Social understand-ing includes:

- The ability to understand, interpret, and respond appropriately in personal and social situations
- The awareness and understanding of what is being said, asked, implied, or expected
- The appreciation of someone else's feelings and reactions: sympa-thy, empathy, the ability to put oneself in another's place
- The understanding of someone else's state of mind: the beliefs, the unstated assumptions, the references, the intentions that another person brings to the situation
- The knowledge of society's codes and conventions

Did you realize that we bring so much knowledge and ability to our own social interactions? Being able to understand, interpret, respond, appreciate, and empathize all require a good deal of know-how and expe-rience. Some children seem to be born with highly developed social abil-ity; they can interact with anyone and elicit smiles wherever they go. Other kids need hands-on intervention in order to develop these skills.

Here are some things parents can do to get their children ready for the variety of social situations they will encounter.

BROADEN YOUR CHILD'S EXPERIENCE

The more knowledge, awareness, and interests the child has, the more ready for conversation and social interaction he/she will be and the more able to figure out what is going on in social situations. So get out that old list from preschool and make sure your child has experienced firsthand a farm, a zoo, the circus, a city, the woods, the fire house, the police station, the post office, the library, a museum, historical sites, a bus trip, a train ride, a boat ride, the barber shop, a hair salon, the car wash, camping, fishing, a pool, a beach, a play, a concert, a movie, an office, a restaurant, different kinds of stores—the bakery, the dry cleaners, a laundromat, the grocery store, a supermarket, a pet store, a music shop. As you visit each site, draw your child's attention to the sights, sounds, smells, and textures that are there to be perceived and interpreted. At first, you'll probably point these things out to your child; later, use these visits to practice your child's getting information for him/herself.

Enroll the child in dance or gymnastics classes, swimming, sports, scouts, religious education—whatever other kids of the same age are doing. Coach the child in advance on how to participate appropriately (perhaps a volunteer could be on hand to assist with this). Make sure your child has at least a passing knowledge of current jokes, movies, TV shows, and music.

LEARNING TO PLAY

Get your child ready for the many structured and unstructured play situations he/she will encounter in the early years. Make sure he/she can take turns and share. Teach the standard ways of playing with toys. For example, if your child likes to turn a car or truck over and just spin the wheels, let him/her know that when playing with others, he/she must run the car along the floor. Watch for overly repetitive motions and work toward expanding the child's play repertoire. Make sure the child has experience with various games and playground equipment.

Some children need assistance in learning to enjoy the company of other children. Try pointing out the pleasant sound of children's laughter and describing to your child the fun the children are having. Create games or pretend situations that will intrigue your child and involve

Table 5.1.   Social Development: The Blind/VI Child Needs to Be Prepared for the Many Situations of Normal Life

Visiting another child's home	Extracurricular activities
Walking to school, the park, home	Board games
Walking in a line	Going to parties
Classroom participation	Shopping
Going through the cafeteria line	Handling money
Lunchtime conversation	Using public bathrooms
Gym exercises, movements, games	Using a phone
Recess	Keeping track of belongings
Active games	Joining a group
Playground equipment	Being a friend without being a burden
Team games	Extracurricular activities

Some Helpful Skills for Good Social Interactions

Nice appearance	Social understanding and judgment
Normal postures and body positions	Conversation skills
Appropriate tone and volume of voice	Independent mobility skills
Good manners and eating skills	Appropriate assertiveness

another child. Once you have the game going, point out to your child how he/she is having fun with the other child.

Teach your child to recognize an invitation to play—the words or physical signals another child might use when trying to start a game or activity. Work on appropriate ways to respond to such overtures. The better your child gets at recognizing and responding to these invitations to play, the more he/she will be included in play activities at school, during recess, and at other children's homes after school or on weekends, and the more fun he/she will have.

Teach your child acceptable ways to react if he/she is annoyed. Make sure your child understands what to expect when he/she annoys others! Teach the child how to tell when others are getting annoyed and to pick up on the signs and words before things get out of hand.

Have children over to your house. It really does take practice to develop social skills, so the more opportunities you provide, the better the chance that your child will develop the skills. At first, you might have to set up the activities and be involved yourself. But as your child develops the ability to interact and have fun with another child, you can recede more and more into the background.

If your child is having trouble relating to peers, it can be helpful to invite children who are a little older or younger to come over to play. The older kids can direct the play and bring your child along and the younger children won't have so many rules and regulations about how the play should go. Both situations can give your child good play experience. Siblings and cousins can fit the bill here, too, as can a mother's helper, an older child whose job it is to play with your child while you are home to keep an eye on things.

DEVELOPING PERSONALITY

As you expose your child to other children, draw your child's attention to what kids say and how they say it, their tone of voice, their joking, their laughter. This is especially important if your child tends to sound more like a little adult than a kid when he/she talks. The more exposure to other children your child has, the more opportunity there will be for him/her to model him/herself after other children instead of after adults. This will help in social interaction with peers.

Flexibility

Another aspect of personality to develop is flexibility. Flexibility will help the child play, socialize, and get along better with peers, teachers, and others with whom he/she interacts. Guide your child toward being comfortable with the changeability of life, especially if he/she tends toward the rigid. Teach your child to have a plan B—and maybe even a C and a D—and not to get upset if plan A doesn't work out. If the child becomes comfortable with the idea that plans sometimes change, he/she will be much more at ease socially when other children change the game or activity. Add flexibility to your child's growing repertoire of play skills, and there will be a better chance of his or her having a successful play date.

Judgment

Good judgment is another element of personality important to develop. Judgment enables a person to decide what is appropriate to say and do in various situations and to determine who is a good and safe person with whom to interact. In the early years, parents can facilitate the development of judgment by creating opportunities for the child to make guided choices. A guided choice is one in which either choice is a good one. For example, the parent might say to a young child, "It's cold outside. Would you like to wear your fuzzy red sweater or your smooth blue

Figure 5.1.　Taking a ride on a sunny day.

one?" As your child gains experience in making simple choices, guide him/her toward the reasoning power that will lead to the ability to make actual decisions. For example, you might say, "Are you very hungry? If you are, you might want to have this big piece of fish. If you're not so hungry, you might want to take a smaller one." Talking through the reasons behind decisions will get your child into the habit of thinking before he/she acts. Eventually all this practice in good decision-making leads to the development of good judgment.

Appropriate Assertiveness

As your child develops judgment, he/she will begin to understand when it is important and necessary to speak up for him/herself. This skill is needed for so many life situations—to get into a conversation, to be heard in a classroom, to be waited on at a store, to ask for help, to fend off overprotection, and many others (more on this in chapter 6). Your child shouldn't be so loud and insistent that people are turned off; but neither should he/she be so passive that people don't even know (or care) that he/she is there.

Figure 5.2. Learning how to a team player.

Don't Talk for Your Child

Attention all parents—especially moms! You'd be amazed at how often parents step in and answer questions that have been addressed to their child. Don't do it! Don't talk for your child. I know there are many reasons that we do it: We're in the habit; we're protecting them; we think they can't handle the question; they don't know the answer or don't know how to respond. It is much more beneficial to the child if, instead of talking for them, we take notice of the question or kind of question or topic, and give the child some practice or coaching at home so that they can more and more speak for themselves in the many and varied situations they will encounter.

Let Your Child Grow Up

There is a certainly a tendency on the part of the sighted world to baby and overprotect the blind/VI child. We parents fall into this trap, too. But it is critical for your child's development that you allow, encourage, and

Figure 5.3.   Hanging out with the kids in the neighborhood.

insist on age-appropriate skills and behavior. For example, don't lift your blind/VI child into the car seat after he/she is able to climb into it him/herself; don't carry your child up or down the stairs if he/she is able to do it; don't let your loving and lovable child hug everyone long after other children of the same age have given up this behavior.

CONVERSATION AND SOCIAL INTERACTION SKILLS

The ability to talk easily with others is a key social skill. Children need to learn about the give-and-take required for conversation, ways in which to get and keep a conversation going, and the various social signals that tell when a conversation is going well and when it needs to end. Here are some tips.

Face the Speaker

Teach your child to face the person he/she is talking to. If the conversation is taking place while people are seated, teach the child to turn his/her head toward the speaker. Sighted people attach a great deal of signifi-

Figure 5.4. A child who has had many experiences will have lots to talk about with friends.

cance to this behavior. Facing the speaker indicates interest and attention. Not facing the speaker is associated with disinterest, a lack of understanding, and rudeness, all things we want our children to avoid, especially if that is not really what is going on.

Respect Personal Space

Teach your child about the idea of not invading personal space. Here's an easy way to demonstrate appropriate space between people. Stand with arms at your side. Then keeping elbows at the waist, bend your arms at the elbow, bringing your hands out in front. If your hands touch another person, you are too close. As your child gains experience, he/she will be able also to use sound to judge appropriate distance. Remind your child that it is generally not appropriate to touch other people while talking to them.

Sometimes children with partial vision come up too close to people trying to get them in view. Useful as that eyesight may be, this is not a good way to employ it, as it can be a real turn-off to others. Provide the partially

Figure 5.5.   One of the gang.

sighted child with alternatives such as those above to handle this kind of social situation.

Appropriate Voice Volume and Tone

Encourage your child to speak with a friendly and expressive tone of voice. Don't let him/her speak too loudly or in such a low voice that others have to make a great effort to hear him/her. Adults may make this effort, but after a while, other kids won't and your child will be ignored (and we don't want the child to get used to being ignored).

Be Interesting and Interested

It takes two to have a conversation and conversation works best when each party is both *interesting* and *interested*. How can you help your child be interesting? Well, you're already working on broadening his/her awareness and experience so that he/she has a variety of things to talk about. Make sure your child understands that conversation is a two-way street. The topic must be of interest to both parties; train your child not to talk incessantly about a topic in which only he/she is interested. Help him/her learn how to figure out if the other person is interested as well (see "How to Tell if You Are Boring Someone" and "How to Tell if Someone Is Enjoying the Conversation," below).

Another key to keeping a conversation going is to be interested in—or at least appear to be interested in—what the other person is saying. A good conversationalist asks appropriate, friendly questions (not nosy or pushy) that show interest in learning more, and responds with comments that are related to what the person has just said and that lead the conversation forward. Coach your child and give him/her opportunities to develop and practice these skills by making up scenarios and having the child think of appropriate responses that move the conversation along.

Teach him/her the little niceties like nodding or saying *mmm-hmmm* at appropriate times to show the person that he/she is listening. If needed, bring your child's attention to facial expressions and practice appropriate and responsive ones.

What and How Much to Say

Conversations work by the participants taking turns, and no one likes to wait too long for a turn. Help your child realize that he/she must not talk too much in each turn. He/she must give the other person a chance or else the other party will get bored pretty quickly. I've heard it said that an appropriate amount of talking for one turn is just about the amount of Braille that would fit on an index card. Perhaps this idea can help your child gauge an appropriate amount to say.

On the other end of the spectrum is the child who seems to have nothing to say and gives only one syllable answers if someone asks him/her a question. It is really important to coach your child at home on the skill of *thinking of something to say*! This is important now and will be important in later life, for example, at that interview for his or her first-choice college. Give your child practice by creating conversation scenarios and coaching him/her in possible replies that would be appropriate and interesting to the other person. See if you can get him/her to the point of being able to think of two or three possible appropriate responses to each scenario. Get his/her brain used to thinking this way!

When to Jump In

Another skill that leads to social interaction is knowing how to join a group and enter a conversation that is already in progress. The child needs to learn when it would be appropriate to jump into a conversation and when it would not be. Much of this knowledge comes from experience, but you can point out the basics to your child to at least get the awareness rolling.

The child should listen a moment to figure out what is going on in the conversation. If the conversation is personal, it would generally not be appropriate (or successful) to attempt to join in. If the conversation seems general, for example, about a sports team that is winning or losing or a test that everyone just took, joining in is usually all right. (As children get older, the social rules become stricter for who is "allowed" to join in conversations and when it would be considered okay and when it would be considered "weird." That's why these ideas are only basics.) One caveat: While listening a moment to figure out what the conversation is about, make sure your child does not appear to be "lurking," a behavior that will look strange and unacceptable to sighted peers.

If people are standing around talking, they are often set up in a loose circle. The child should learn how to get into a circle, using listening skills to align him/herself correctly. Perhaps you can use family gatherings, where there will be less social pressure, as a time for your child to learn this skill. It does take practice, but it's an important skill to have for social situations with peers. Children will be more apt to exclude a child who is situated in some inappropriate position, and to include a child who gets into the circle in the usual way.

Another skill related to group conversation is the timing of comments. It can be a little tricky to wait long enough to make sure a person has finished speaking but not so long that another person starts talking and the child never gets his/her comment in. This is another skill that can be practiced in family situations where there is less social pressure.

Make sure your child understands that, generally speaking, he/she can't change the topic when joining a group conversation. The idea is to go with the flow. If he/she has something to say that is related to the topic at hand, that is fine, but the child must not blurt out a comment on a subject that is completely unrelated to the conversation or that only he/she is interested in.

Be Aware of the Effect You Are Having on Others

The next key is to pay attention to what happens after the child joins the conversation. If the conversation continues and the child is included in it, then *bingo*, the child is having a successful social experience. But what if the conversation pretty much stops after the child jumps in?

How to Tell If You Are Boring Someone

This may seem brutal, but our kids need to recognize when they are boring someone. Some of the signs of boredom are: only a minimal response from the other person—nothing that continues the conversation or moves it forward; a lot of "ah-ha's" or "mmm-hmmm's"; no response at all; the person looks for the first chance to end the conversation; the person disappears as soon as the child stops talking; the person avoids the child.

People lose interest when they are bored; they stop paying attention and may completely stop listening. They may even get to the point where they avoid the child at all cost. Adults may humor a child for a while, but peers almost certainly won't. *We don't want our kids to get used to this minimal level of social response.* If being ignored becomes their social norm, their expectation, they will not progress and develop their social skills. This is not the road that leads to better social interaction; instead, it leads to learned passivity, strange habits, and increased isolation. Instead, we want the child to learn new ways to participate in conversation, ways which the child will realize result in a much more fun and rich experience.

Interventions

Being aware of one's effect on others is not an easy task for young children, and we do not want to make our children overly self-conscious; however, if there is a problem in this area, we do need to bring our children's attention to it. Parents can be the ones who initially take note of what is happening in unsuccessful social encounters. Initially, we can analyze what took place and make suggestions for change. Eventually, we want the child to be able to do this.

Think More about the Other Person

One technique is to teach the child to think more about the other person than him/herself (this is another area where social understanding comes in). Teach, coach, and tutor the child and give him/her lots of practice in thinking about what might be going on in the other person's mind. For example, in a practice conversation, make a minimal response and have the child figure out what that means you might be thinking or feeling. In another conversation, give a response that keeps the conversation moving along. Do this many times in order to get your child into the habit of thinking about the other person's response. Give the child practice in thinking up something interesting or relevant to say. Then, in the next real situation when you hear the old pattern emerging, you can find some subtle way to remind the child to employ his/her new techniques. Keep practicing with your child until you notice that the boredom issue is no longer or very rarely occurring. Once your child is aware of the social signals and picks up on them, social interaction is bound to improve.

How to Tell if Someone Is Enjoying the Conversation

Signs of a conversation going well are: mutual laughter; an even give-and-take of comments; the other person asks questions that indicate an interest in hearing more; the person contributes comments of his/her own related to what the child has said in order to keep the conversation going; the other person stays and continues the conversation even though he/she could find a reason or an excuse to walk away.

Recognizing When Someone Is Walking Away

Make sure your child recognizes when someone is walking away. Although the typical advice on the basics of visual impairment tells the sighted person to let the blind/VI person know when he/she is departing, it's even better if the blind/VI person learns to recognize it for him/herself. In this way, your child will not end up holding the person there while the person is trying to move away and will also not find him/herself in the embarrassing position of talking to the air.

Conversation Skills Summary

The general do's and don'ts for conversation can be summarized as follows: Be flexible, responsive, interested, and interesting. Continue and expand on the subject, don't change it to your own. Don't talk too much; don't just give yes/no or one syllable answers. Note how the other person is responding in order to judge if the conversation is going well. The better a person is at picking up on and understanding the subtleties of the situation, the better he/she will be at choosing a response or subject that will be successful. Be alert to the signals that indicate when a conversation needs to come to a close. It's much better to leave a person wanting more than wanting to get away!

RELAXED POSTURES AND POSITIONS

Look around the next time you are in a room with a bunch of children. Observe the positions they are in. Are they seated symmetrically with their feet on the floor and their hands in their laps? Or are they more leaning on the table or sprawled across the sofa? If you have a child who tends to sit or stand a bit stiffly in just one position, introduce him/her to the variety of positions a person can take. Especially work on the ones that look informal and relaxed, as these are the postures and positions that bespeak confidence and invite social interaction. Some examples are sitting with elbow/s up on the table and chin resting in hand/s; sitting with forearms leaning on the table; sitting side saddle on a chair with arm over the back of the chair; standing leaning against a wall with one knee bent; standing as in the previous example with one knee bent and foot crossed over the other ankle; placing one or both hands on hips; arms folded.

Don't forget to encourage your child to smile. People who smile look confident and relaxed.

Encourage Socially Acceptable Postures and Behaviors and Extinguish Inappropriate Ones

Here's the bottom line: Stand up straight. Head up! Face the person you're talking to. No rocking, no fists in eyes, no fingers in mouth, no flicking hands, no head rolling around. Be careful about touching other people, no mouthing of objects. Generally speaking, no jumping up and down.

If your child is engaging in inappropriate behavior, try to figure out the reason why. Is he bored? Does she need to get out some excess energy? Give your child something more interesting and fun to do with his/her hands and mind than repetitive movements and going off into his/her own world. Find socially acceptable ways and times for your child to vent that excess energy—running, jumping on a trampoline, using a hippity-hop toy, learning gymnastics moves. Explain what looks okay visually and what does not. When in the company of others, you can use a subtle sign to remind your child to stop a behavior, such as a snap of the fingers. Some parents find it effective to limit an inappropriate behavior by telling the child he/she can indulge in it only at certain times or in certain locations.

It's not easy to extinguish these habits if your child has them; however, keep working at it. These behaviors *will be* a barrier to social interaction if they keep up; substituting socially acceptable ones will mean much more social opportunity for your child.

APPEARANCE

A clean, relatively in-style appearance will help your child blend in with peers. At age-appropriate times, your child should take responsibility for showering and washing hair (more on this in Chapter 3: Independent

Living Skills). While you are still in charge of choosing clothing for your child, select styles that are age-appropriate so that he/she fits in. As time goes on, your child will decide on his/her own style.

MANNERS AND EATING SKILLS

Having good manners, like having good conversation skills, involves thinking about the other person. We need to be alert and responsive to the ways our behaviors affect others. We say "thank you" if someone has done something nice for us; we say "you're welcome" to acknowledge someone's thanks. We are expected to keep our elbows off the table while we eat and keep our mouths closed while we chew. Our society's codes demand that we excuse ourselves if we burp in public, interrupt, or bump into someone. Teach your blind/VI child all the usual manners that you would teach any of your children. Age-appropriateness is again the key.

A few specifics are in order for blind/VI kids. Some children, often through no fault of their own, get so accustomed to being waited on or helped that they end up with the attitude that the world owes this to them. They expect everyone to do things for them. They don't say "please" and "thank you"; they don't say "excuse me" when they touch someone with their cane. This will not go over well with peers. Don't let this happen to your child.

Eating skills is another area that may call for special attention by parents of blind/VI kids. Eating is, among other things, a social activity. Make sure your child has decent eating skills so that he/she will be welcome by other children to share a meal in the school cafeteria (more on this in Chapter 3). Eating skills are really important for now and for the future—for a date, a meal at a boyfriend or girlfriend's house, dinner in the college dining hall, a business lunch.

And, speaking of business lunches, make sure your child—whether a boy or a girl—develops a firm handshake and knows how long to keep the gesture going before letting go.

HANDLING LIFE SITUATIONS

Make sure your child learns the alternative skills of blindness/visual impairment that lead to independence, competence, and confidence. A child who can confidently and competently handle the various situations that life presents—school, family, and social life—will be attractive to others and will have an easier time socially. The skills of blindness/visual impairment will enable your child to be an equal participant in social outings, to be a friend without being a burden.

In fact, raise your child with the expectation that he/she will not always be on the receiving end of help, but will make a contribution to others. As your child gains skills and competence, he/she will internalize the idea that he/she can contribute and function on terms of equality with sighted peers.

TEACHING OTHERS

There are several things that parents can do when their child is young to develop awareness among peers, teachers, neighbors, family members, and others. Start by learning positive ways to talk about blindness/visual impairment and the abilities of blind/VI people. If anyone expresses sadness or pity toward your child, help them understand that the skills and tools of blindness/visual impairment will enable your child to participate fully in life. Briefly explain your child's study methods and mobility techniques. Treat blindness/visual impairment matter-of-factly. Don't make a big deal about it. Blindness/visual impairment is just one of your child's characteristics. Speak openly about blindness/visual impairment. Don't discuss it in hushed tones or behind the child's back. It's nothing to be ashamed of, nothing to hide. It's okay to be blind/VI.

Work toward others viewing your child in terms of equality and not as someone who is always in need of help. Look for opportunities in which your child can do something to help others.

In addition to instructing the blind/VI child in social interaction skills, parents can also give tips to sighted peers. Explain that your child may not see body language or gestures and that the best way to get his/her attention is to use his/her name. Encourage them to teach your child playground protocols and games. Point out that games can be modified to include sound cues. Get everyone thinking, "How can we get a blind/VI kid into this game?"

Make your home an inviting place, where children will want to come to play and hang out. Bake cookies, make popcorn, have interesting things to do. Take a friend along on family outings.

Teachers Can Help

Teachers, too, can play a role in facilitating social interaction.

Social Interaction: How Teachers Can Help

- Be committed to facilitating social interaction;
- Consider social-emotional development a major focus, especially in the younger grades;

- Include social-emotional, self-help, and language-communication skills in the curriculum, especially for younger children;
- Create an environment in which individual differences are valued;
- Promote understanding and respect for all;
- Promote positive self-concept, healthy attitudes, and independence in all children;
- Use teaching and classroom management strategies that include all children, promote group socialization, and encourage interaction and friendships;
- If there is an aide in the classroom, make sure the presence of the aide does not interfere with the blind/VI child's social interaction with peers;
- Explain and interpret behaviors for both blind and sighted students;
- Teach children how to initiate and respond to interaction;
- Verbalize and prompt social exchanges; and
- Intervene when necessary.

LOOKING DOWN THE ROAD

Look down the road toward the future and think about where you would like your child to be in terms of social ability. Then make sure your child is on the road that leads there. Continue to give your child practice in all the social skills, as it is practice that leads to mastery, competence, and confidence. By using a variety of techniques—guidance, modeling, role playing, coaching, direct instruction, feedback, and signals—and providing your child with repeated exposure to social situations and long-term practice, you will put him or her on the road not only to social competence but to enjoying life and having a lot of fun with peers.

CHAPTER 6

DEVELOPING
SELF-ADVOCACY SKILLS

The Pursuit of a Normal Life

INTRODUCTION

Rounding out the set of skills your child will need for a successful launch
into an independent future are self-advocacy skills. Self-advocacy is the
ability to effectively speak for—and speak up for—yourself. The long-
term goal is for our children to be able to take charge of their own lives
and not need or expect others to speak for or be responsible for them.
The process leading to this goal begins in early childhood and continues
over the years in age-appropriate steps. At first, parents do the advocating—we protect, support, advocate for, and, when necessary, fight for our
children. Then, little by little, the balance shifts as we teach and empower
our children to advocate for themselves and insist that they receive
opportunities for increasing independence. As we train our children to
step forward, we ourselves learn to step back.

POSITIVE ATTITUDE AND POSITIVE LANGUAGE

To be effective self-advocates, our children need to feel comfortable with
all aspects and characteristics of themselves, including their blindness/

*Getting Ready for College Begins in Third Grade: Working Toward an Independent Future
for Your Blind/Visually Impaired Child*, pp. 87–91
Copyright © 2010 by Information Age Publishing

visual impairment. One way to develop this comfort level in your child is to learn and use positive language about blindness/visual impairment and the abilities of blind/visually impaired people. Seek out competent blind/VI people who can serve as mentors and role models for your child and read the stories of accomplished blind/VI professionals.

Unless you live in a large city, your child is probably the only blind/VI student in the school system, and there is a good chance that school personnel have not had experience with blindness/visual impairment. Parents can use this situation as an opportunity to teach high expectations and positive attitudes and language to others.

In the meantime, your child will be watching and listening. Positive attitudes and language will ensure that your child sees him/herself as a whole and complete human being, not as a collection of deficits and needs, as sometimes is the view in the education and medical systems. As your child hears you speaking positive words, he or she will feel good about him/herself both as a person and as a blind/VI person and will begin to internalize the message: It's okay to be blind. Blindness is just one of many characteristics that make up who someone is. Blindness/visual impairment does not stop a person from achieving goals.

DEVELOPING COMPETENCE

Most definitions of self-advocacy focus on the person's understanding his/her disability, knowing his/her needs, and knowing how to request accommodations. For a blind/VI person, the more important focus is *acquiring the skills to get the job done* and *effectively communicating to others how he or she will accomplish the task*. Don't think in terms of having things done for the child or making things easier for him or her; instead, think about the child's knowing how to do things. In other words, don't think *accommodations*; think *skills*.

Life Experiences

One of the foundations for developing competence is having many, many experiences with the people, places, and things in the world. As an active participant in the world, your child will learn how to interact with others, find out how things work, develop a store of knowledge comparable to sighted peers, and learn how to do things. As understanding and ability grow, your child will learn to make comparisons, make choices, and make decisions. All these lead to the development of judgment, a very important component of self-advocacy skills and being able to care for oneself.

Skills of Blindness/Visual Impairment

So many of the people your child will encounter in the world will make the automatic and immediate assumption that your child needs help. Your job is to make sure your child learns the alternative skills of blindness/visual impairment that will enable him/her to handle age-appropriate tasks, demonstrate that help is not needed, and earn the respect of those around him/her. Blind/VI children need the ability to accomplish the normal tasks of life in the normal amount of time. Be sure that your child learns all the alternative skills needed to complete schoolwork independently, travel in and around the school building and in your neighborhood independently, do his/her fair share of household chores, and otherwise complete all the tasks expected of a child his or her age. Expose him/her to the variety of tools and options that exist for getting any particular job done.

Special Alert for Parents of Partially Sighted Children

It is very common for parents of partially sighted children to feel relieved that their child "is not blind." Teachers might say the child is lucky that he/she "won't have to" learn Braille or "won't have to" use a cane. The child is encouraged to use his/her remaining vision for all tasks and is rewarded by making Mom and Dad happy when he/she is able to see. Perhaps the child even feels embarrassed or ashamed if he/she is unable to accomplish a task visually.

Typically, these children are not taught the alternative nonvisual skills and are expected to function entirely visually. Until, that is, their impaired vision is unable to manage a particular task. Then these children start receiving accommodation after accommodation—shortened assignments, recorded books, someone to take notes for them, someone to accompany them on class trips, someone to get them safely from class to class. If these children have internalized the idea that being able to see is good and pleasing to adults, but having difficulty seeing is bad and makes the adults feel sad, and if they feel embarrassed or self-conscious about not seeing well enough to keep up, then *they will not be inclined to speak up for themselves* when their vision alone is not sufficient for the task at hand. Given "accommodations" that actually shortchange them by not empowering them to do the work, left without alternative skills to accomplish the task, and not having the advocacy skills to speak up, these children truly are helpless. Is this any preparation for an independent future?

Don't let this happen to your child! Make sure that instead of "accommodations," he/she is given the opportunity to gain age-appropriate skills. Instead of assistance, make sure he/she is provided with the tools that lead to empowerment and independence. Then, instead of feeling frustrated or embarrassed, or seeing him/herself as in need of help or protection, your child could view him/herself as—and really be—a competent, equal participant in the world.

DEVELOPING CONFIDENCE

As your child gains experience and skill, he or she will also be building confidence and self-assurance. You can encourage the development of confidence through the atmosphere you create in your home.

- Encourage your child to be active, not passive. Teach him/her not to allow others to constantly handle, move, and manipulate him/her.
- Don't answer when your child is asked a question. Let your child speak for him/herself.
- Respect your child's opinion.
- Encourage appropriate assertiveness; encourage a shy child; rein in one who is too forward.
- Encourage a confident voice and appropriate volume; again, encourage a child with a tiny, timid voice, and tone down one whose voice is too loud. Coach your child in this area if needed and have him/her practice speaking in an appropriate voice.
- Encourage your child to express his/her needs appropriately.
- Teach your child to say a polite but firm "no, thank you" when help is not needed.

The Necessary "No, Thank You"

Blind/VI children (and even adults) are vulnerable to the unasked-for and often unwanted "assistance" of innumerable well-intentioned people who, without thinking to ask, will pull them, push them, move them, steer them, place them, decide for them, and on and on. People will always be "protecting" your child, automatically assuming that they—by virtue of having eyesight—know what that blind/VI person needs. If your child does not gain the ability to deal effectively with these situations when they occur, he/she will be kept from having a normal, self-directed life.

Most books on blindness/visual impairment or disability talk about the ability to speak up to tell others your *needs*. I believe for blind/VI people, the speaking up is much more needed to protest what you *don't need*! Cultivate in your child the ability to speak up for him/herself when these situations occur. Empower him or her to say a polite but firm "no, thank you" to unwanted assistance, accommodations, or special treatment.

Remember that the ability to say a realistic "no, thank you" is predicated on the child's actually having the experience, judgment, and skills to handle the task him/herself.

Social Interaction Skills

Whether trying to arrange an accommodation, request assistance, or avoid unwanted help, your child needs the social interaction skills to make him/herself understood and to persuade others to do what he/she wants. Practice ways to ask for and refuse things that will result in the desired outcome.

HANDING OVER THE REINS

As your child heads toward the beginning of high school, the balance will be shifting and he/she will begin taking on the responsibility of advocating for him/herself. Secure in your love and support, bolstered by your belief in him/her, becoming skilled in decision-making and judgment, filled with confidence and the competence to back it up, and fortified by the belief that he/she deserves equal treatment, your child will be well on the way to becoming an effective self-advocate, ready for increasing independence and the challenges of the next exciting phase of life.

APPENDIX

RESOURCES FOR FAMILIES

National Organization of Parents of Blind Children (NOPBC)
http://www.nopbc.org
The National Organization of Parents of Blind Children (NOPBC) offers support, information, training, and advocacy to families and teachers of blind/VI children. A division of the National Federation of the Blind, NOPBC offers the unique advantage of providing families and teachers opportunities to network with and be mentored by competent blind/VI adults.

National Parents Seminar and Conference
http://www.nopbc.org
Every year since it was established in 1983, the NOPBC has conducted an annual seminar for parents and teachers of blind/VI children as a part of the National Convention of the National Federation of the Blind (NFB). The program has grown to include five exciting days of workshops; training sessions; activities for all family members, including sighted siblings; and countless opportunities to meet other families and children from around the country.

State/Regional Conventions and Seminars
http://www.nopbc.org
State Parents of Blind Children (POBC) organizations in collaboration with state NFB affiliates offer seminars, workshops, training sessions, and

educational and social activities for families, children, and youth in the various states and regions.

Future Reflections Magazine
http://www.nfb.org/nfb/Future_Reflections.asp
The national magazine *Future Reflections* provides resources and information on topics related to the education and development of blind/VI children from birth through college. With its positive philosophy about blindness, the magazine is a vital source of support and encouragement to parents and teachers. Special editions are available on the topics of "The Early Years," "Braille," "Cane Travel & Independence," "Low Vision & Blindness," "Sports & Fitness," and "Let's Talk about Blindness"—an issue designed especially for our kids. *Future Reflections* is published quarterly and distributed free of charge in print, online, and in recorded form by the American Action Fund for Blind Children and Adults in partnership with the National Organization of Parents of Blind Children.

NOPBC Website
http://www.nopbc.org
The website of the National Organization of Parents of Blind Children is packed with information that will assist parents and teachers as they raise and educate their blind/VI children. The site includes special sections for new parents; education; IEP help; resources; links to the national magazine *Future Reflections*; and ways to connect with other parents in your state and across the country.

Literature and Information Packets
http://www.nfb.org/nfb/information_packets.asp?SnID=1183785616
http://www.nfb.org/nfb/Literature.asp?SnID=1098444533
This literature provides information and inspiration for parents and teachers of blind/VI children. Topics include early childhood, the blind/VI child in the elementary classroom, independent mobility, IEPs, social skills, and many others.

Books and Videos
http://secure.nfb.org/ecommerce/asp/prodtype.asp?prodtype=14
http://www.nfb.org/nfb/Kernel_Books.asp
http://www.nfb.org/nfb/NOPBC_Books.asp?SnID=1098444533
This collection of books and videos will raise expectations and provide a how-to for families and teachers as they raise and educate their blind/VI children. Titles include *The Bridge to Braille, Making It Work, Independent Movement and Travel in Blind Children, Avoiding an IEP Disaster, White Canes for Blind Kids, Handbook for Itinerant and Resource Teachers,* and many more.

Blindkid and Other Listservs

http://www.nfbnet.org/mailman/listinfo/blindkid_nfbnet.org
http://www.nfbnet.org/mailman/listinfo/nabs-l_nfbnet.org

Want to talk about your blind/VI kid with other parents? Would you like tips from knowledgeable blind/VI adults? Ask questions, get and give advice, vent frustrations, brag about your kid, share resources, and make new friends on this NOPBC sponsored listserv. To subscribe, visit the link above and fill out the form provided on the page. Other lists that might be of interest to you and your child include blind/VI students, blind/VI math, music, art education, blind/VI journalists, blind/VI teachers, blind/VI cooks, blind/VI wheelchair users, guide dog users, crafters and artists, performing artists, and various state parent lists.

Braille Reading Pals Club

http://www.nfb.org/nfb/Braille_Reading_Pals_-_Early_Literacy_Program
.asp

Braille Reading Pals is an early literacy program that encourages parents to read daily with their blind or low vision children, ages 0–7 (or older if the children have developmental delays), who are not yet reading. Sponsored by the NFB Jernigan Institute and the NOPBC, this free program runs throughout the year.

Early Childhood Conferences

http://www.nfb.org/nfb/Beginnings_Blueprints.asp

The NFB Jernigan Institute in collaboration with the NOPBC periodically holds innovative Beginnings and Blueprints Early Childhood Conferences. These two-day conferences bring together families of blind/VI children, ages birth to seven, with early childhood service providers, teachers, and blind/VI adults in order to raise expectations, provide training, and enhance the early childhood experience of blind/VI children.

Pop-Up IEP

http://www.unco.edu/ncssd/bviIEP/index.shtml

A resource to help parents advocate for blind/VI students in the IEP process. Includes issues that typically arise, effective responses, and pertinent quotations from the law.

Braille Readers are Leaders Contest

http://www.nfb.org/nfb/Braille_Readers_Are_Leaders_Overview.asp

This literacy program, co-sponsored by NOPBC and the National Association to Promote the Use of Braille (NAPUB), features a Braille reading contest for blind/VI children grades K-12, special recognition to schools for the blind that promote Braille literacy, and Community Service

Awards for blind/VI students who use their Braille skills to give back to others.

Slate Pals

http://www.nfb.org/nfb/NOPBC_Slate_Pals.asp?SnID=2

Slate Pals is a free pen-pal program for children aged 6–18 from around the world. Slate Pals enables children who are blind/VI to correspond with one another in Braille. It also finds blind/VI pen pals for sighted children who are interested in learning the Braille code.

AAF Free Books Program

http://www.actionfund.org/actionfund/
Free_Braille_Books.asp?SnID=1563301384

This free books program sponsored by the American Action Fund for Blind Children and Adults (AAF) provides popular books each month in Braille to blind/VI children.

ShareBraille

http://www.nfbsharebraille.org

NFB ShareBraille was developed to facilitate the exchange of Braille books through a community-run library. NFB ShareBraille helps connect those who are looking for materials in Braille with those who have Braille books to donate.

Writing Contests

http://www.nfb-writers-division.org/

Sponsored by the NFB Writers Division, this contest invites blind/VI youth to enter original stories and poetry and compete for cash prizes and a chance for publication in the NFB Writers Division magazine, *Slate and Style*.

Junior Science Academy

http://www.blindscience.org/ncbys/
Junior_Science_Academy_Mentor_Info.asp

The 4-day sessions of the Junior Science Academy introduce blind and low-vision children from 8 to 12 years old to the excitement of science in real-life applications. Through hands-on instruction, field trips, and interactive activities taught by blind scientists, students learn that science can be fun as they participate in challenging experiences focused on earth and physical sciences. Parents and guardians accompanying their children to the program attend workshops provided in partnership with NOPBC.

Youth Slam

http://www.blindscience.org/ncbys/Default.asp

This bi-annual STEM (Science, Technology, Engineering, and Mathematics) program for high-school students, ages 14–18, empowers blind and low-vision youth through hands-on activities and challenging experiences led by blind scientists in areas such as green engineering, architecture and design, astronomy and aeronautics, chemistry, computer science and artificial intelligence, crime scene investigation (CSI), physics, and robotics. The event includes social and recreation opportunities.

National Center for Blind Youth in Science

http://www.blindscience.org/ncbys/default.asp?SnID=1498703842

This national clearinghouse provides resources, information, and expertise for blind/VI youth in science, technology, engineering, and math (STEM) subjects and careers. Specific information is available for biology, chemistry, physics, geometry, et cetera. Partners include the National Science Foundation, the National Aeronautic and Space Administration (NASA), and other leading organizations.

National Association of Blind Students (NABS)

http://www.nfb.org/nfb/NABS.asp

NABS provides support, information, and encouragement to blind/VI high school and college students. NABS offers information on national testing, accessible textbooks, technology, and more.

NFB-Newsline

http://www.nfb.org/nfb/Newspapers_by_Phone.asp

Lifetime learning and ready access to current information and events is part of what makes a good citizen, a successful student and employee, and a valuable participant in community life. NFB-Newsline is a free service that enables eligible individuals to receive newspapers and magazines over the telephone or via email twenty-four hours a day, seven days a week. The service offers over 300 newspapers, including five Spanish-language papers, and many magazines, such as *Popular Science* and the *Smithsonian*. NFB-Newsline enables blind/VI children to complete current events assignments on their own and do their homework independently.

Blindness 411

Blindness 411 was created by the National Federation of the Blind to give blind/VI teens a place to meet other teens and learn about resources for school, home, and community. Current Facebook members can go to groups, search for Blindness 411, and request access to the group.

Scholarship Program
http://www.nfb.org/nfb/scholarship_program.asp
Each year, the National Federation of the Blind gives a broad array of scholarships to recognize achievement by blind/VI scholars. To be eligible for a scholarship, students must be legally blind in both eyes, must reside in the US, the District of Columbia, or Puerto Rico, must be pursuing or planning to pursue a full-time, postsecondary course of study in a degree program at a U.S. institution of higher learning, and must participate in all scheduled scholarship program activities at the NFB Convention. High-school seniors and those already in college or graduate school may apply.

Straight Talk About Blindness Series
http://www.nfb.org/nfb/Straight_Talk.asp?SnID=1557929868
This Web-based video series, hosted by the Executive Director of the NFB Jernigan Institute, focuses on issues surrounding blindness and visual impairment.

ABOUT THE AUTHOR

Carol Castellano is the author of *Making It Work: Educating the Blind/Visually Impaired Student in the Regular School* and *Because Books Matter: Reading Braille Books with Young Blind Children* and co-author of *The Bridge to Braille: Reading and School Success for the Young Blind Child*. Her work has been recognized internationally and appears on blindness services websites of countries around the world. Carol makes presentations for parents and teachers across the country and has served as an advisor for the Teacher of the Blind/Visually Impaired Program at The College of New Jersey. She currently serves as president of the National Organization of Parents of Blind Children and president of Parents of Blind Children-NJ. Carol's daughter, totally blind and now a young adult, is a college graduate.

INDEX